D0376682

MANAGING
DIVERSE
CLASSROOMS

ASCD MEMBER BOOK

Many ASCD members received this book as a
member benefit upon its initial release.

Learn more at: **www.ascd.org/memberbooks**

MANAGING
DIVERSE
CLASSROOMS

HOW TO BUILD
ON STUDENTS'
CULTURAL
STRENGTHS

CARRIE ROTHSTEIN-FISCH
ELISE TRUMBULL

ASSOCIATION FOR SUPERVISION AND CURRICULUM DEVELOPMENT
ALEXANDRIA, VIRGINIA USA

Association for Supervision and Curriculum Development
1703 N. Beauregard St. • Alexandria, VA 22311-1714 USA
Phone: 800-933-2723 or 703-578-9600 • Fax: 703-575-5400
Web site: www.ascd.org • E-mail: member@ascd.org
Author guidelines: www.ascd.org/write

Gene R. Carter, *Executive Director;* Nancy Modrak, *Publisher;* Julie Houtz, *Director of Book Editing & Production;* Leah Lakins, *Project Manager;* Georgia Park, *Senior Graphic Designer;* Keith Demmons, *Typesetter;* Sarah Plumb, *Production Specialist*

Copyright © 2008 by the Association for Supervision and Curriculum Development (ASCD). All rights reserved. No part of this publication may be reproduced or transmitted in any form or by any means, electronic or mechanical, including photocopy, recording, or any information storage and retrieval system, without permission from ASCD. Readers who wish to duplicate material copyrighted by ASCD may do so for a small fee by contacting the Copyright Clearance Center (CCC), 222 Rosewood Dr., Danvers, MA 01923, USA (phone: 978-750-8400; fax: 978-646-8600; Web: www.copyright.com). For requests to reprint rather than photocopy, contact ASCD's permissions office: 703-575-5749 or permissions@ascd.org. Translation inquiries: translations@ascd.org.

Printed in the United States of America. Cover art copyright © 2008 by ASCD. ASCD publications present a variety of viewpoints. The views expressed or implied in this book should not be interpreted as official positions of the Association.

All Web links in this book are correct as of the publication date below but may have become inactive or otherwise modified since that time. If you notice a deactivated or changed link, please e-mail books@ascd.org with the words "Link Update" in the subject line. In your message, please specify the Web link, the book title, and the page number on which the link appears.

ASCD Member Book, No. FY08-4 (January 2008, PC). ASCD Member Books mail to Premium (P) and Comprehensive (C) members on this schedule: Jan., PC; Feb., P; Apr., PC; May, P; July, PC; Aug., P; Sept., PC; Nov., PC; Dec., P.

PAPERBACK ISBN: 978-1-4166-0624-6   ASCD product #107014
Also available as an e-book through ebrary, netLibrary, and many online booksellers (see Books in Print for the ISBNs).

Quantity discounts for the paperback edition only: 10–49 copies, 10%; 50+ copies, 15%; for 1,000 or more copies, call 800-933-2723, ext. 5634, or 703-575-5634. For desk copies: member@ascd.org.

Library of Congress Cataloging-in-Publication Data

Rothstein-Fisch, Carrie.
  Managing diverse classrooms : how to build on students' cultural strengths / Carrie Rothstein-Fisch and Elise Trumbull.
     p. cm.
  Includes bibliographical references and index.
  ISBN 978-1-4166-0624-6 (pbk. : alk. paper) 1. Multicultural education--United States. 2. Classroom management--United States. I. Trumbull, Elise. II. Title.

  LC1099.3.R68 2008
  371.102'4--dc22

                              2007036782

18 17 16 15 14 13 12 11 10 09 08   1 2 3 4 5 6 7 8 9 10 11 12

To all our colleagues in education whose innovations make the most of their students' cultural strengths.

MANAGING DIVERSE CLASSROOMS

HOW TO BUILD ON STUDENTS' CULTURAL STRENGTHS

ACKNOWLEDGMENTS

In addition to fresh ideas and high motivation, writing a book requires numerous other resources. Among them are a goodly supply of optimism, a deep well of patience, and an enormous amount of collegial support. Like any book, this one is the result of many people's efforts. Our Bridging Cultures colleagues have sustained us on all counts. First among these colleagues is Dr. Patricia Marks Greenfield, whose visionary work in the field of culture and human development underpins this book and the project on which it is based. The Bridging Cultures® Project was a direct outgrowth of her research with her colleagues Dr. Catherine Raeff and Dr. Blanca Quiroz, and her leadership in the project cannot be overstated. It is particularly fitting that Dr. Greenfield has written the Foreword to the book, setting the tone and context for the representation of a body of work that owes so much to her.

Dr. Blanca Quiroz, who was a graduate student at the inception of the Bridging Cultures Project, is a founding research partner of the project along with us and Dr. Greenfield. Her insights, grounded in her personal bicultural experience as well as theory, have guided us throughout the life of the Bridging Cultures Project. Her participation has continued throughout her graduate study at UCLA, her pursuit of a doctorate at Harvard, and her first years as an assistant professor at Texas A&M University.

We are profoundly grateful to the Bridging Cultures teachers, who began as participants in our workshops on culture, human development, and education and then became co–researchers in their own classrooms and schools. They are Ms. Marie Altchech, Ms. Catherine

Daley, Mrs. Kathy Eyler, Mrs. Elvia Hernandez, Mr. Giancarlo Mercado, Mrs. Amada Pérez, and Ms. Pearl Saitzyk. These exceptional teachers have shown exquisite skill in interpreting and applying theory as well as continuously reflecting upon and refining their practices. Their innovations and thinking are at the heart of this book. All of these teachers were generous enough to share both successes and failures and to make their thoughts and actions explicit for others to learn from. We also thank their cooperating schools and administrators, who allowed them to try innovations within their classrooms and permitted us to observe.

Appreciation is due to colleagues who have encouraged us to write this book, in particular Dr. Beverly Cabello, Dr. Janet E. Fish, Dr. Rie Rogers Mitchell, and middle school teacher Mrs. Sharon Schneider. We are especially appreciative for the comments and insights on our manuscript from kindergarten teacher Mrs. Angela Werth. We believe that feedback from educators at many points in the grade continuum has strengthened the book.

Abundant thanks go also to our editors at the Association for Supervision and Curriculum Development, Ms. Carolyn Pool and Ms. Leah Lakins. They have been unfailingly generous with their time and support, and we have found their guidance astute. It has been an immense pleasure to work with both of them.

Writing a book is inevitably taxing on the authors' families, who can never be given as much credit as they deserve. To our husbands Bryan Fisch and Jerry Salzman, we are immeasurably grateful for your patience and understanding and for demonstrating your respect for what it takes to write a book by taking on endless additional tasks of daily life. To our children, thank you for being flexible about "family time."

The Bridging Cultures Project was initially supported by a grant from the U.S. Department of Education, Office of Educational Research and Improvement to WestEd, the regional laboratory for the Western United States. This grant funded Elise Trumbull to manage the project. WestEd holds the Bridging Cultures® trademark and has licensed its use to the four founding Bridging Cultures researchers: Patricia M. Greenfield, Blanca Quiroz, Carrie Rothstein-Fisch, and Elise Trumbull. We thank the Russell Sage Foundation for its support for the writing of this book, through a grant to Patricia M. Greenfield. Additional financial support from California State University, Northridge, has supported the first author to collect much of the data presented here and to prepare the final manuscript.

FOREWORD

My mentor Jerome Bruner was fond of saying, "Nothing is so practical as a good theory." *Managing Diverse Classrooms: How to Build on Students' Cultural Strengths* by Carrie Rothstein-Fisch and Elise Trumbull proves his point. Starting with a theory of two cultural pathways of development—one collectivistic, the other individualistic—Rothstein-Fisch and Trumbull demonstrate that teachers can use a theoretical paradigm to generate manifold ways to manage a classroom in culturally compatible ways.

When Elise Trumbull was at WestEd in San Francisco, she had the vision to see the potential of our research, showing that a cross-cultural conflict in values between Latino immigrant families and the schools was the heart of the problem of formal education for the families' children. Elise contacted me about our research that documented this conflict in preschool and elementary school, and a collaboration was born. Carrie Rothstein-Fisch, from California State University, Northridge, immediately joined us, contributing her professional expertise in preservice teacher training. This is the team that has produced this tremendously useful and important volume, making culture and cultural diversity the heart of classroom management for the very first time.

Managing Diverse Classrooms not only shows the value of theory for the practical everyday needs of teachers, it also shows what teachers can do with empirical research. When we gave our first workshop, we found that teachers had an "aha!" experience when our research findings showed them that parents had different goals for child development than they did. For example, they learned that helping one another was a very high priority for Latino immigrant parents, whereas, in the same situation, teachers favored independent achievement. Before that, most had assumed that there were right and wrong ways to do things at school and with the school. They had never realized that what was right from the school's perspective could be very wrong from the parents' perspective.

From this "aha!" experience, as readers will see, Bridging Cultures teachers forged a partnership with us that has lasted to this day, more than 10 years later. The teachers began to use their understanding of the two cultures to develop new classroom management practices; their practices became our research findings and "results," a most unusual but rewarding type of research. It was rewarding because the ongoing development of new practices showed that the training had "stuck" and it showed its generativity in producing classroom changes ranging from increased parent involvement to modifications in class procedures and rules. It is these practices that *Managing Diverse Classrooms* documents and shares with other teachers and educators who may experience the same clash of cultures in school settings.

In today's test-heavy environment, these results are not necessarily considered to be important "effects." However, I believe that Bridging Cultures will be the Head Start of this decade—a key factor for keeping Latino immigrant children in school. They will stay in school because Bridging Cultures will allow them to do so without losing respect for or distancing themselves from their parents. Children from Latino immigrant families, Native American children, or children from other collectivistic backgrounds will not have to make an either/or choice between two value systems because their schools will show, through the classroom management practices revealed in this book, respect for the collectivistic value system they often bring with them. Bridging Cultures classroom management is a bedrock on which scholastic achievement can rest within multicultural schools.

Patricia Greenfield
Venice, California

INTRODUCTION:
THE NEED FOR A NEW APPROACH

Unlike other books on classroom organization and management, this book examines the topic from a cultural perspective. Our premise is that cultural values and beliefs are at the core of all classroom organization and management decisions. In parallel fashion, cultural values and beliefs are at the center of students' responses to teachers' strategies and of students' own attempts to engage in and influence interactions in the classroom.

Books and articles on classroom organization and management have only recently begun to address the role of culture. But when culture *is* addressed in the literature, it tends to be from the perspective of encouraging teachers to recognize cultural differences in parents' orientations to child rearing and schooling. Teachers may be led to examine culture from the perspective of the outsider (that is, "*Those* people have culture") but not to regard themselves as people whose values and beliefs are inherently cultural. However, schools and teachers have cultures too (Hollins, 1996; Lipka, 1998).

School culture is relatively consistent across the United States and reflects the individualistic values of the dominant, European American culture. For instance, students are expected to show respect for others and their personal property, to stay in assigned seats, and to keep their hands to themselves (Marzano, 2003). They are supposed to be responsible for their own individual learning, even as members of cooperative groups (Slavin, 2006). Parents are encouraged to participate in their children's schooling in certain ways, such as helping with homework, volunteering in the classroom, or attending schoolwide events

(Connors & Epstein, 1995). For students, certain kinds of culture-based communication styles are sanctioned over others, especially in discussions of subject matter (Morine-Dershimer, 2006). Likewise, teachers' approaches to classroom organization and management also reflect cultural values, usually those of the mainstream institutions in which they have been schooled (see Lipka, 1998).

One model that recognizes the role of culture is described in the article "Culturally Responsive Classroom Management" (Weinstein, Curran, & Tomlinson-Clarke, 2003). The authors identify three components for achieving culturally responsive management: (1) recognition of one's own cultural beliefs, biases, and assumptions; (2) acknowledgment of others' ethnic, cultural, and other differences; and (3) understanding of the ways that "schools reflect and perpetuate discriminatory practices of the larger society" (p. 270). These are essential elements for culturally responsive classroom management, but realizing them can be a daunting task for teachers. They need to know *how to* (1) examine their own cultural values, (2) develop understanding of the values of others and regard them in a nonjudgmental way, and (3) apply what they learn about cultural differences to the improvement of classroom practices, particularly in a way that is meaningful, nonthreatening, and not overwhelming.

THE BRIDGING CULTURES APPROACH

This book attempts to address the *how to* of building on students' cultural strengths in the realm of classroom organization and management. First, we explore a framework for understanding culture that focuses on the most important and fundamental differences between two types of cultural orientations—individualistic and collectivistic. In individualistic cultures, the emphasis is on the growth and development of the individual as an increasingly independent entity who learns to meet his or her own needs. In collectivistic cultures, the emphasis is on the growth and development of an individual who remains closely connected to his or her family and makes its well-being a priority. (Chapter 1 provides more detail about the differences.) Second, we show how teachers used the individualism/collectivism framework to understand their own cultural values and those of their school as well as those of the children and families they serve. Third, we provide many examples of how teachers put their new understanding to use in order to improve classroom organization, teaching, and learning.

We believe an uncomplicated framework that captures the most basic ways that cultures differ is far more useful than lengthy lists of the features of various cultures. Teachers, whose roles and responsibilities have become increasingly complex and demanding, could hardly be asked to remember all those details! Moreover, our research with teachers shows that the individualism/collectivism framework (described in Chapter 1) is immediately understandable and useful both for teachers' self-reflection and as a way to understand children and families. Ultimately, it is a vehicle for finding common ground.

Our approach and the teacher innovations presented throughout this book are compatible with a sociocultural, constructivist, and developmental view of learning as opposed to a behaviorist one. From our perspective, the organization and management of the daily life of the classroom should reflect understanding of the following:

• Students are active learners whose development takes place within particular social and cultural contexts and is influenced by those contexts.
• Home socialization practices influence how students interact and solve problems.
• Good classroom organization and management tap existing skills and dispositions while building new capacities.
• As they mature, students can take increasing responsibility for regulating their own learning and ensuring harmony in the classroom.

THE BRIDGING CULTURES PROJECT

Our model for approaching classroom organization and management is based on a unique combination of theory, research, and teacher-constructed practices. Working with colleagues Patricia Greenfield and Blanca Quiroz, we developed the Bridging Cultures Project, a collaborative action research project.[1] The project emerged from empirical research demonstrating the presence of cultural values conflicts in schools (Greenfield, Quiroz, & Raeff, 2000; Raeff, Greenfield, & Quiroz, 2000) and a theory of cultural differences (Greenfield, 1994; Hofstede, 2001; Markus & Kitayama, 1991; Triandis, 1989). Seven elementary school teachers who work with large numbers of immigrant Latino students and their families became teacher-researchers; they learned about the individualism/collectivism framework and then used that framework as a guide for designing culturally informed instructional strategies that made sense for their classrooms.

The result of the seven teachers' efforts is a mountain of innovation: a collection of strategies and ideas for classroom organization and management that are completely field-tested by teachers who have come to understand the central role of culture in learning and teaching. The teachers did not set out to explore classroom management, yet it became the first thing that they changed as a result of their new understanding of the cultural values of their students. New organizational strategies were integral to these changes in management. As we observed teachers over a period of five years, met with them semimonthly, and conducted individual interviews with them, we came to see that classroom organization and management were among the elements most strongly influenced by teachers' knowledge of cultural differences (see Trumbull, Diaz-Meza, Hasan, & Rothstein-Fisch, 2001).

THEMES OF THE BOOK

This book has several themes—big ideas that rise to the surface on the basis of many examples. Readers may discover additional themes, but the following seemed particularly salient.

Teachers as Cultural Brokers

When teachers have models for understanding cultural differences, they can create classroom organization and management from the

[1] Bridging Cultures is a registered trademark of WestEd. All rights reserved.

inside out instead of responding only to students' external behaviors and guessing what might be going on inside their minds and hearts. Teachers who are knowledgeable about the culture of school and the cultures of their students can serve as "cultural brokers," helping their students and students' families negotiate new cultural terrain and become biculturally proficient (Cabello & Burstein, 1995; Delgado-Gaitan, 1996). They can also share their cultural knowledge about families with other school personnel and help to influence the development of policies that are more culturally congruent for families.

Teachers Constructing Their Own Strategies

The Bridging Cultures Project did not have a compendium of strategies up its sleeve for teachers to learn and implement. In fact, no strategies—none whatsoever—were recommended to teachers. The idea was that, given a useful framework and some provocative research results, these capable, motivated, experienced teachers were likely to design their own strategies to make their classrooms more hospitable for their students. We still believe that nothing is as practical as a good theoretical framework that gets teachers observing, thinking, reflecting, and devising new practices that make sense in their own professional contexts.

Making the Implicit Explicit

One problem with differences in cultural values is that they tend to remain implicit—invisible—and hence a source of conflicts that may never get satisfactorily resolved. Children whose home values conflict with school values may become very confused as to what is "appropriate behavior." When parents instruct children to listen quietly and not "bother" the teacher, for instance, the teacher may think the children are shy or limited in English proficiency. A teacher who understands that such students may have been socialized at home to be quiet and respectful is likely to both interpret and act on the students' behavior in a different way, one more aligned to what the real reasons are behind the students' apparent lack of oral participation.

Listening to Teachers' Voices

The innovations from Bridging Cultures teachers are the heart of this book, and many of them are presented in the teachers' own words. Teachers' voices are not filtered to achieve a consistent editorial style. The examples of practice presented in the book are teacher-designed, field-tested practices designed by real elementary school teachers to better serve their largely immigrant Latino student populations. The level of insight exhibited by the teachers as they digested the research and theory and experimented with new practices in their classrooms was impressive. And their synergistic exchanges when they met as a group were incredibly rich with ideas on topics such as the use of small-group activities, monitors, discipline, family communication, and the organization of instruction and assessment. It is fair to say that the four professional researchers were impressed at the quantity and quality of the teachers' insights and changes in practice!

The data we cite come from classroom observations and field notes, in-depth interviews, notes from group meetings, videotapes, and informal conversations (in person, by phone, and via e-mail). Through these varied means, we believe we have accurately captured the thinking and practice of the seven dedicated educators with whom we worked. We cite the teachers by name because they have served as colleagues and researchers in their own right rather than anonymous subjects in the project.

Implementing Innovations in Homogeneous Versus Heterogeneous Classrooms

In the majority of the Bridging Cultures classrooms, students were from immigrant Latino populations, and although teachers reported that many were born in the United States, the data available to us suggest that few of their parents were. In some classrooms, all of the students were Latino; other classrooms included some African Americans and a few European Americans. Thus most of the students were from collectivistic cultures. (Latin American cultures tend to be far more collectivistic than the dominant, European American culture [Hofstede, 2001]. African American culture, too, is more collectivistic than the dominant culture, though it has been described as also having some strong individualistic elements [Boykin & Bailey, 2000; Nelson-LeGall & Resnick, 1998]).

Overall, the practices described throughout this book reflect a turn away from the individualistic practices of most classrooms. The intent is not an effort to eliminate them completely, but to bring them into balance with the collectivistic practices of the homes of the students.

When teachers in more heterogeneous classrooms try out some of the practices we offer, the results may differ from those observed in Bridging Cultures classrooms. Teachers will need to consider what mix of organizational and management strategies work best for their students. Nevertheless, it would be difficult to argue that collaboration, helping, and sharing are not important for all students. At the same time, some students may need explicit coaching on how to work more collaboratively. It is likely that in culturally heterogeneous classrooms some mix of individualistic and collectivistic strategies will be most effective. Even the Bridging Cultures teachers do not use exclusively collectivistic organizational and management strategies, as mentioned, because they believe their students need to be able to learn to operate in an individualistic society as well as in a collectivistic family. They wish to develop a bridge that facilitates learning in both directions.

The key to making good decisions about organization and management, as we emphasize, is to develop an awareness of the important values of school and home cultures so as to avoid putting students in the position of choosing one system over the other. This tension was identified by one of our Bridging Cultures teachers, Mrs. Amada Pérez, who was born in Mexico. Speaking of herself and her siblings, she said,

> [We came to feel that] the rules at school were more important than the rules at home. The school and the teachers were

right. As a child, you begin to feel the conflict. Many of my brothers stopped communicating with the family and with my father because he was ignorant. (Rothstein-Fisch, 2003, p. 20)

THE ORGANIZATION OF THE BOOK

Chapter 1 introduces the individualism/collectivism framework and key concepts related to classroom organization and management. Chapter 2 shows how the "power of the group" is drawn upon to maintain a focus on instruction and a harmonious interpersonal environment. Chapter 3 discusses how classroom organization and management can be built upon knowledge of families' cultural value systems and how this allowed Bridging Cultures teachers to vastly improve home-school relations. Chapter 4 shows how students' values and skills of helping and sharing were tapped to keep classrooms humming with meaningful learning activities. Chapter 5 gives many examples of how classroom management, or "orchestration," was accomplished through strategies that relied on students' collectivistic values. Chapter 6 deals with the organization of learning in the content areas, with special attention to language arts and mathematics. Chapter 7 addresses classroom orchestration as applied to student assessment. Finally, the Conclusion examines several important issues, including new directions for classroom orchestration and recommendations for future research.

It has been challenging to organize this book into discrete chapters because new ways of thinking about classroom organization and management are integral to many aspects of educational programs. In addition, the cultural strategies that teachers have used are interrelated and integrated throughout their instructional programs. For example, collaborative group work, helping, and sharing—all compatible with students' collectivistic values—often occur simultaneously and can apply to many aspects of instruction. Thus the same example may appear in several places in the book, but can be analyzed with regard to different issues.

Two additional points of clarification may help readers. First, it is important to know that over the five years of the project teachers' assignments occasionally changed, though they remained at the elementary school level. We cite the grade level in many of our examples, but to avoid redundancy, we have purposely omitted it where it doesn't seem as critical to the example. Second, when we cite an example of a practice or an extended teacher quotation that has been published previously, we give the published source. When a quotation is not attributed, it comes from our field notes, observations or group meetings, interviews, or videotaped workshops.

A NEW WAY OF THINKING ABOUT CLASSROOM MANAGEMENT

Teacher 1: "I'm having real problems with my class. They keep helping each other when I want them to work independently. They touch each other, can't seem to keep their materials to themselves, and every time I ask them a question about a fact, they answer with a story about their family!"

Teacher 2: "It must be a cultural thing."

Teacher 1: "What does culture have to do with classroom management? I have to get the kids to behave and learn!"

What does culture have to do with classroom management? As it turns out, it has *a lot* to do with it! The goal of *Managing Diverse Classrooms* is to look at the impact of culture on classroom organization and management. Throughout this book, we examine how teachers equipped with a framework for understanding cultural differences have constructed novel ways of organizing their classrooms.

One of the most common concerns of teachers is how to manage a classroom full of students (Evertson & Weinstein, 2006). After all, if the classroom is in chaos, how can learning take place? In this book, we suggest that, in order to make good decisions about classroom organization and management, teachers need to understand the role of culture in human development and schooling. Understanding the role of culture does not mean learning endless facts about a great many cultures, but rather coming to see how culture shapes beliefs about learning and education. When teachers understand cultural differences, they begin to re-examine and redesign their classroom organization and management in many fruitful ways (Trumbull, Rothstein-Fisch, Greenfield, & Quiroz, 2001). As a result, teaching and learning become easier.

In this chapter, we lay the foundation for the innovations described throughout the book. We briefly define classroom management and culture so as to be explicit about what we mean by our terminology. In particular, we describe the intersection of classroom management and culture. Next, we introduce the individualism/collectivism framework—the system for understanding cultural differences that underlies all the innovations described throughout the book. Finally, we describe two important studies that demonstrate how cultural value systems of individualism and collectivism can influence school settings.

WHAT DO WE MEAN BY *CLASSROOM MANAGEMENT?*

In Figure 1.1 we define the terms used throughout the book. Both *classroom organization* and *classroom management* have the ultimate goal of making the classroom environment hospitable for learning. We agree with Weinstein's (2003) observation that "the fundamental task of classroom management is to create an inclusive, supportive, and caring environment" (p. 267). Organization, especially the social organization that includes how students communicate and interact with each other and the teacher, is also a key to an inclusive, supportive, and caring environment. Every choice a teacher makes about organization or management reflects a cultural perspective, whether it is visible or not. Likewise, the teacher's choices will affect students in different ways, depending upon how the children have been socialized within their home cultures. Thus, "effective classroom management requires knowledge of cultural backgrounds" (Weinstein, 2003, p. 268). Such knowledge is essential also to the development of caring relationships and the interpersonal skills needed to interact effectively with both students and their families.

FIGURE 1.1

Classroom Management Terms

Classroom management—the set of strategies that teachers and students use to ensure a productive, harmonious learning environment to prevent disruptions in the learning process

Classroom orchestration—the processes of structuring classroom interactions and activities in ways that harmonize values of home and school, drawing on students' cultural resources to resolve problems, avoid conflicts, and minimize the need for discipline

Classroom organization—the ways that teachers structure classroom interactions and activities to promote learning, including communication, relationships, time, and the arrangement of the physical environment

Discipline—any action or set of actions taken by the teacher to directly control student behavior (a component of management)

Punishment—a form of discipline entailing either withdrawing a privilege or subjecting the student to unpleasant consequences

WHAT DO WE MEAN BY *CULTURE?*

What, exactly, is *culture?* Our way of thinking about culture has been called a "cognitive" approach to culture because we are interested in the deep elements of culture related to thinking, teaching, learning, and making meaning (Fetterman, 1989). We define *culture* as "the systems of values, beliefs, and ways of knowing that guide communities of people in their daily lives" (Trumbull, 2005, p. 35). The concept of "systems of values and beliefs" is central to what we describe later in this chapter—the cultural values framework that has proven effective in helping teachers learn about two differing cultural values systems. By "ways of knowing," we mean how people organize their world cognitively through language and other symbol systems. It includes how they approach learning and problem solving, how they construct knowledge, and how they pass it on from generation to generation. Culture is manifest in how groups of people carry on in their daily lives. For example, some people like to stay together as a family for all kinds of weekend activities, whereas others prefer to "do their own thing." These are not just matters of personal preference, but are guided by cultural values, as we will see.

HOW IS CULTURE INVOLVED IN ORGANIZATION AND MANAGEMENT?

Questions of organization and management are, ultimately, questions of what is valued in a particular setting (Evertson & Randolph, 1995, p. 19). What happens in the classroom is primarily reflective of the cultural values of the school and the teacher. For example, "[w]hat teachers consider to be 'discipline problems' are determined by their own culture, filtered through personal values and teaching style" (Johns & Espinoza, 1996, p. 9). Of course, there are differences in teachers' instructional and management styles (Walker & Hoover-Dempsey, 2006), but the underlying values motivating teachers' behaviors are likely to be quite similar. This similarity results from two observable facts: (1) the majority of teachers are European American and implicitly hold dominant-culture values (Gay, 2006); and (2) most "other" teachers have been educated in U.S. schools, and in that process, they have been taught "the right way" to teach and manage the classroom. For this reason, teachers from nondominant cultural groups have often learned to suppress their intuitive cultural knowledge in favor of the "best practices" that they learned in school (Hollins, 1996; Lipka, 1998; Trumbull et al., 2001).

THE BRIDGING CULTURES PROJECT

The examples that fill these pages come from the Bridging Cultures Project, a collaborative action research project involving seven elementary school teachers in classrooms with large numbers of immigrant Latino students. Unlike most teacher training interventions that are short term, the Bridging Cultures Project has been a longitudinal professional development and research endeavor. The project began with three professional development workshops completed in four months, and it continued with a series of whole-group meetings, classroom observations, and interviews over a period of five years. Although the project is described in detail elsewhere (Trumbull, Diaz-Meza, Hasan, & Rothstein-Fisch, 2001), readers of this book will benefit from knowing about the participants, the school's demographics and contexts, and the Bridging Cultures approach to classroom organization and management.

Participants

Professional researchers. Four professional researchers collaborated to develop and carry out the project: Dr. Patricia M. Greenfield, a professor of Cross-cultural Psychology at the University of California, Los Angeles; Dr. Greenfield's graduate student, Ms. Blanca Quiroz (now Dr. Quiroz is an assistant professor at Texas A&M University); Dr. Carrie Rothstein-Fisch, associate professor of Educational Psychology and Counseling at California State University, Northridge; and Dr. Elise Trumbull, an applied linguist and, at the time, senior research associate with WestEd, the regional educational laboratory based in San Francisco.

Teacher-researchers. The seven teachers in the Bridging Cultures Project were all teaching in bilingual (Spanish-English) elementary school classrooms and had an interest in multicultural education. They all had ample teaching experience, ranging from 5 to 21 years, with an average of 12.7 years. Four of the teachers are Latino, and three are European American. Two teachers were born in Mexico, one in Peru, and one in Germany, although all of these four had immigrated to the United States between the ages of 2 and 8. The other three teachers were born in the United States. Six teachers are female, and one is male.

As a fortuitous bonus, the teachers represented all grade levels from kindergarten through 5th grade, and this remained true throughout the project, even with changes in grade assignments for the first four years. Three of the teachers have master's degrees (two in education, one in fine arts), and two were highly involved in the Los Angeles Unified School District's Intern Program as mentor teachers.

During the course of the project, two teachers earned their National Board for Professional Teaching Standards Certification. These were *not* average teachers! However, they were perfect candidates to help us understand and apply the framework of individualism and collectivism to educational practice in the real world. We use the teachers' real names throughout this book because it contains *their* teaching and learning innovations. They are Marie Altchech, Catherine Daley, Kathy Eyler, Elvia Hernandez, Amada Pérez, Giancarlo Mercado, and Pearl Saitzyk.

The participant selection process deserves some description. Teachers were recruited specifically because they were identified as being interested in learning more about their Latino students. We mindfully selected teachers committed to bilingual and multicultural education (and willing to give up three Saturdays for a modest stipend) in schools serving a large student population of poor immigrant Latino students from Mexico and Central America. Experience with this particular population turned out to be very important because evidence indicated that immigrants from these areas might be among the most collectivistic students in the United States (see Goldenberg & Gallimore, 1995; Greenfield, Quiroz, & Raeff, 2000; Raeff, Greenfield, & Quiroz, 2000; Valdés, 1996). This fact would increase the likelihood that knowledge of the individualistic and collectivistic systems would provide teachers with an immediate context for applying new content knowledge to a population that might benefit most. Our hypothesis was that if the framework were useful for committed teachers working with a population who had experienced conflict in cross-cultural values, then they would be able to construct meaningful new classroom practices based on their knowledge of the competing cultural values systems.

School Demographics and Contexts

The seven teachers taught at six different schools. All the schools are in Southern California: five teachers taught at four schools in the Los Angeles Unified School District (LAUSD), one teacher taught in Ventura County (about 60 miles north of Los Angeles), and one teacher taught in the city of Whittier (in southern Los Angeles county). The teacher from Ventura County taught at a school where a vast majority of students came from immigrant or migrant farm worker families. These children lived in the most rural area, and because of the association of collectivism with rural residence and an agricultural way of life, we consider them to be the most collectivistic of all of our classroom groups. Two of the seven teachers taught in one of the lowest-performing schools in Los Angeles, based on standardized test scores. Two other schools were located in high-crime, urban neighborhoods.

Approach to Classroom Organization and Management

Overall, the purpose of the project was to foster culturally responsive teaching and learning opportunities for immigrant Latino students and their families, the population served by the participating teachers. The project used a cultural values framework to see if teachers' understanding of the deep meaning of culture would have implications for teaching and learning.

The Bridging Cultures Project emphasized two things: (1) supporting teachers to deepen their knowledge of cultural values systems and the role of those systems in human development, schooling, learning, and teaching; and (2) offering teachers an opportunity to adopt "a self-reflective stance whereby the contribution of their own attitudes, values, and taken-for-granted cultural patterns" (Bowers & Flinders, 1990, p. 7) and those of their schools can be examined. It was this combination of a powerful but accessible cultural theory and the innovations of the Bridging Cultures teachers that motivated us to write this book.

Many teachers feel frustrated and overwhelmed when it comes to acquiring cultural knowledge. Describing her perspective before she participated in the Bridging Cultures Project, Mrs. Eyler said

I wanted to understand my students better, so I started studying Mexican culture. Then I realized that the children in my class came from so many distinct regions of Mexico, Central and South America, each with differing histories and traditions. I knew that I would never know enough. I had to give up trying.

Though many teachers may have had at least some opportunity to learn about cultural issues in education, whether through preservice courses or professional development workshops, they are not likely to have had access to a theoretical framework that is both easy to grasp and immediately useful for understanding arguably the most important distinctions among cultures. The individualism/collectivism framework is just that. We have come to call it the "Bridging Cultures framework," but in truth sociologists and anthropologists have seen the explanatory power of the framework for more than 50 years—although they have not always used the labels "individualism" and "collectivism" (Waltman & Bush-Bacelis, 1995).

Using this streamlined framework, with only two elements, the Bridging Cultures teachers were able to generate an almost endless array of successful strategies for working with the students and families they served. The framework and the examples we present should stimulate readers to generate their own innovations that make sense in their particular school communities. In fact, the framework is most useful when it is used as a guide to learn from students and families directly about the details of their own lives.

INDIVIDUALISM AND COLLECTIVISM: TWO CONTRASTING VALUE SYSTEMS

Research suggests that two broad cultural value systems, individualism and collectivism, shape people's thoughts and actions in virtually all aspects of life (Greenfield, 1994; Hofstede, 2001; Markus & Kitayama, 1991; Triandis, 1989). Figure 1.2 lists some of the most important contrasts between individualism and collectivism.

The fundamental distinction between these two systems is the relative emphasis placed on individual versus group well-being. "While self-realization is the ideal with many individualistic cultures, in the collectivist model, individuals must fit into the group, and group realization is the ideal" (Waltman & Bush-Bacelis, 1995, pp. 66–67). It is not a matter of valuing one or the other—individual or group—but rather the degree of emphasis accorded to each.

FIGURE 1.2

The Individualism/Collectivism Framework

Individualism	Collectivism
Representative of mainstream United States, Western Europe, Australia, and Canada	Representative of 70% of world cultures (Triandis, 1989), including those of many U.S. immigrants
Well-being of individual; responsibility for self	Well-being of group; responsibility for group
Independence/self-reliance	Interdependence/cooperation
Individual achievement	Family/group success
Self-expression	Respect
Self-esteem	Modesty
Task orientation	Social orientation
Cognitive intelligence	Social intelligence

Before proceeding further, we caution once again that every culture has both individualistic and collectivistic values. The dichotomy we present is a distillation of the "general tendencies that may emerge when the members of . . . [a] culture are considered as a whole" (Markus & Kitayama, 1991, p. 225). Great variation exists within a culture, just as any one person will exhibit both individualistic and collectivistic behaviors at different times. The elements that constitute culture are not separate and static but rather interactive and constantly evolving (see Rogoff, 2003; Shore, 2002). Of course, within any cultural group, individuals will vary in the degree to which they identify with particular values, beliefs, or ways of knowing. Yet it can be very useful for teachers to understand the dominant tendencies of a cultural group as a starting place for exploration and further learning. We return to these points later in this chapter.

In the United States, a country known for its history of "rugged individualism," the dominant values include independence, self-reliance, individual achievement, and cognitive development. Children learn early on that they are expected to take responsibility for themselves first and foremost, and it is regarded as a healthy developmental step when young adults achieve separation from their families (Hofstede, 2001). The individualistic American views himself as someone who is "a distinct individual . . . capable of self-assertion and . . . free to think and act according to personal choice or volition" (Raeff, 1997, p. 225). Common proverbs capture this individualistic world view: "Stand on your own two feet." "Every man for himself." "The squeaky wheel gets the grease."

In contrast, children from collectivistic families are socialized with values that emphasize working together *interdependently* rather than working alone *independently* (Greenfield, 1994). In Mexico, a highly collectivistic country, the dominant values are interdependence, cooperation, family unity, modesty, respect, and social development (Delgado-Gaitan, 1994; Greenfield, 1994; Tapia Uribe, LeVine, & LeVine, 1994). Personal choices are likely to be evaluated relative to their potential benefit to the family, respect for elders, and modesty about one's accomplishments. These choices are valued over self-expression. When it comes to completing a task, it is far more important to engage social relationships first, and then the task will get done (Hofstede, 2001).

Once again, we can look to popular proverbs for insights into what a society values. Consider how the following proverbs reflect a collectivistic perspective: "No task is too big when done together." "Many hands make light work." "The nail that sticks up gets pounded down."

According to Greenfield (1994),

> Each society strikes a particular balance between individual
> and group. The major mode of one society is the minor mode
> of another. The balance is never perfect. Each emphasis [indi-
> vidualism or collectivism] has its own psychological cost. . .
> [I]n socially oriented societies, the cost of interdependence
> is experienced as suppression of individual development,
> whereas in individualistically oriented cultures, the cost of
> independence is experienced as alienation. (p. 5)

Hence, both systems have advantages and disadvantages.

INDIVIDUALISM AND COLLECTIVISM AT SCHOOL

Schools in the United States tend to reflect the values of the dominant culture, which has its roots in Western Europe. They are highly
individualistic, with the goal of teaching children to become independent and to strive for individual success (Greenfield, Quiroz, &
Raeff, 2000). In contrast, many immigrant families (as well as American Indians, Alaska Natives, Pacific Islanders, and African Americans)
socialize their children to be more collectivistic. In their child-rearing
practices, these families emphasize maintenance of close bonds to
family, responsiveness to family needs and goals, and working on
tasks together as a group. In a large study encompassing 72 countries, Hofstede (2001) found that

> [t]he purpose of education is perceived differently by indi-
> vidualist and collectivist societies. In the former, education
> is seen as aimed at preparing the individual for a place in
> society of other individuals. This means learning to cope with
> new, unknown, unforeseen situations . . . [T]he purpose of
> learning is not so much to know *how to do as it is how to
> learn* . . . In the collectivist society, education stresses adapta-
> tion to the skills and virtues necessary to be an acceptable
> group member. This leads to a premium on the products of

tradition. Learning is more often seen as a one-time process, reserved for the young only, who have to learn *how to do things* in order to participate in society. (p. 335)

From the individualistic perspective, learning is an individual matter; knowledge is acquired or constructed by individuals—albeit in a social context. Students are considered responsible for their own learning, and one of the developmental goals of schooling is to foster independent, autonomous learners (Betts, 2004; Centre for Promoting Learner Autonomy, 2006). The learning relationship is primarily between the teacher and the child, not among the group of students in the classroom. If students need help, they ask the teacher questions—something dominant-culture parents often encourage their children to do. Even when students work in cooperative-learning groups, the emphasis is on individual learning and achievement; students receive individual grades based on their contribution (Slavin, 2006). In U.S. schools, academic progress is measured frequently through individual assessment and reported through individual grades. (It is easy to assume that autonomy and collectivism cannot coexist. But members of collectivistic cultures do have autonomy. The individual makes choices, but always voluntarily in cooperation with others. As Mosier and Rogoff [2003] note, small children in Japan or among the Maya in Guatemala may not be urged to help, but they see everyone else helping, and eventually they are likely to choose to help.)

Children from collectivistic families are socialized to work toward group rather than individual goals. They may be accustomed to working together as a group to help others with their tasks even before they consider their own assignment (Raeff, Greenfield, & Quiroz, 2000). Collectivistic families also emphasize learning embedded in a social context. In the classroom, collectivistic students help each other, and group success rather than individual achievement is the goal (McLaughlin & Bryan, 2003). When such students are placed in cooperative-learning groups, they collaborate easily. They have learned to rely on and support each other, and they have been taught not to bother the teacher with questions because that could show disrespect (Valdés, 1996).

From the individualistic point of view, an academic task has value in and of itself. In the classroom, the most important thing is to get one's work done. Relationships with other students come second. But given all that we know about the collectivistic value system, it is not surprising that students from collectivistic backgrounds may be confused when their teacher tells them to pay attention to the task at hand to the exclusion of their peers (Isaac, 1999). In their minds, the relationships are paramount, and academic tasks can be completed much more easily if they help and are helped by each other.

Schooling itself, even in collectivistic societies, is intrinsically individualistic in the sense that achievement is ultimately measured on the individual level. However, the individualism associated with formal education is moderated by the indigenous collectivism in countries such as Mexico (McLaughlin & Bryan, 2003), Japan (Lewis, 1995), and Israel (Ben-Peretz, Eilam, & Yankelevitch, 2006).

Educación Versus Education

An illustration of the differences between collectivistic and individualistic orientations is the meaning of *education* in the United States versus the meaning of *educación* in Spanish. In the United States, education typically refers to formal education in school settings. It is associated with doing well academically and demonstrating that ability through good grades.

For immigrant Latino parents, the purpose of *educación* is much broader: to produce a good and knowledgeable person, one who respects other people and does not place self above others in importance (Valdés, 1996). Social and ethical development and cognitive and academic development are seen as integrated rather than separate (Goldenberg & Gallimore, 1995). One's social behavior in a group (such as the family or the classroom) is of paramount concern; in fact, being a respectful contributor to group well-being rather than focusing on one's own achievement is highly valued. So when immigrant Latino parents come for a parent-teacher conference, their first question is likely to be *"¿Cómo se porta mi hijo/hija?"* ("How is my son/daughter behaving?"). A teacher may find it difficult to stifle her consternation after hearing the same question from 25 or 30 sets of parents, believing that all the parents care about is their child's behavior, when the teacher's goal is to discuss the child's academic progress.

RESEARCH ON GROUP VERSUS INDIVIDUAL ORIENTATION

Two empirical research studies have contributed important insights into how individualism and collectivism operate in the classroom. The first study (Raeff, Greenfield, & Quiroz, 2000) demonstrated that helping in the classroom can be viewed very differently, depending upon one's cultural value orientation. Fifth-grade students, their mothers, and predominantly European American teachers in two schools responded to a series of short scenarios depicting home-school conflicts. In one scenario, a classroom dilemma was posed:

> It is the end of the school day, and the class is cleaning up. Denise isn't feeling well, and she asks Jasmine to help her with her job for the day, which is cleaning the blackboard. Jasmine isn't sure that she will have time to do both jobs. What do you think the teacher should do? (p. 66)

The parents and children sampled in School One were all European American, and they tended to agree with the teachers that in the case of cleaning the blackboard, a third person (such as a volunteer) should be sought. They reasoned that Jasmine had her own job to do, and her first responsibility was to complete her own task. This response illustrates an individualistic value, a primary focus on task completion over social relationships or the welfare of others. It also emphasizes the importance of choice: whether or not a person wants to help is an individual decision.

School Two served immigrant Latino students and their families. An overwhelming majority of immigrant Latino parents (74 percent) selected a "helping" response to solve the dilemma, believing that the first obligation is to help others regardless of one's own individual responsibility to complete a task. In contrast, only 13 percent of the teachers responded with a "helping" solution. Similar to School One, the teachers believed that finding a third person or protecting the task's completion was most important. The students' response to help (36 percent) demonstrates that they are being socialized in the direction of the teachers and away from their parents.

What do these outcomes mean? European American students, parents, and teachers responded very similarly, representing a harmony between home and school for the students in School One. But School Two showed a dramatic difference between the Latino parents on the one hand, and their children and children's teachers on the other. The cultural value of helping, so central to the collectivistic family, was being undermined by the school's individualism. By 5th grade, the students, already becoming products of their U.S. schooling, responded more like their teachers to this scenario. Thus the value of helping that was so important to parents had already begun to lose its potency, and the resolution of conflict between home values and school values shifted toward the value system of school.

In a second study, Greenfield and colleagues (2000) videotaped a series of naturally occurring parent-teacher conferences between immigrant Latino parents and their children's European American elementary school teacher. Discourse analysis of the conversations during conferences revealed that parents and their child's teacher agreed on developmental goals only one-third of the time. More often than not, parents fell silent or changed the subject. The teacher exhibited frustration with the ways parents responded to her comments, and she, too, steered the conversation away from topics the parents brought up. It was evident that the teacher and parents were not understanding each other—not in terms of actual words but in terms of their expectations for the child. The areas of conflict in the discourse tended to cluster around the following themes:

• **The individual versus the family accomplishment**—"[T]he teacher's criterion for positive development was individual accomplishment; the parents' criterion was the accomplishment of the family as a whole or the child's contribution to family accomplishment" (p. 104).

• **Praise versus criticism**—The teacher tended to praise the students (and their accomplishments, to promote self-esteem), whereas parents appeared to avoid praise in favor of criticism (to encourage normative behavior—that is, not sticking out from the group).

• **Cognitive skills versus social skills**—Parents were typically more interested in their children's social behavior, whereas the teacher preferred to discuss cognitive and academic skills. In addition, when the teacher did talk about a social behavior such as talking to other students in class, she evaluated it negatively. "However, it would not necessarily be seen as negative by the parents, who might, from a more collectivistic perspective, view this form of behavior as a way to strengthen social ties among the class members" (p. 105).

• **Oral expression versus respect for authority**—The teacher considered talking in class to be valuable not only for language development but also for cognitive development. Collectivistic parents, on the other hand, tended to want their children to show respect for authority through quiet listening, thus the lack of positive response to the teacher's comments from the parents in the study. In fact, in 26 out of 28 cases, the teacher's suggestion that the students talk more was met with a noncooperative response from the parents. Parents often simply disconnected from the portions of the conversation related to that topic.

• **Parenting role versus teaching role**—The teacher advocated that parents teach their children at home, whereas the parents likely believed that academic instruction was solely the teacher's job. In 21 out of 22 times the topic came up, parents either did not respond or changed the topic. Nor did parents respond positively to the teacher's advice on parenting skills. They seemed to believe that it was their job to parent and the teacher's job to teach. The researchers suggest that perhaps "parents prefer to socialize their children in their own way at home because of a sense that the teacher's suggestions undermine rather than support their ideal child" (p. 106).

Taken together, these two studies by Greenfield and colleagues demonstrate that parents and teachers may often have opposing goals for children from immigrant Latino families, and these differences may cause many kinds of tension and conflict. On the one hand, teachers are interested in task completion, cognitive development, and speaking out. On the other hand, parents seem to value social skills (such as helping and sharing), noncognitive aspects of intelligence, and respect for authority. Guess who is caught between these two sets of conflicting values? As we mentioned in the Introduction (p.xix), this tension is described by Bridging Cultures teacher Amada Pérez:

> [We came to feel that] the rules at school were more important than the rules at home. The school and the teachers were right. As a child, you begin to feel the conflict. Many of my brothers stopped communicating with the family and with my father, because he was ignorant." (Rothstein-Fisch, 2003, p. 20)

No child should have to choose between family or school values and thereby lose out on crucial socialization. But how can optimal learning take place when students are conflicted about what is "right"? Recognition of this cultural tension is the impetus for this book, because when teachers act as cultural brokers, all kinds of harmonious learning and classroom organization can take place.

THE LIMITATIONS OF THE BRIDGING CULTURES FRAMEWORK

Generalizations are risky, and dichotomous lists of cultural features can be misleading on many grounds. In the case of generalizations, naïve or incorrect inferences may be made about groups or individuals, whose histories and lives are always more complex and varied than any framework can capture. Or, as Raeff (1997) puts it, we must bear in mind that common values may "be played out in different specific forms . . . , shaping different goals and routes of self-development" (p. 228). So, for instance, the collectivism of Korean Canadians (Kim & Choi, 1994) will look different from that of Mexican Americans (Delgado-Gaitan, 1994).

In the case of a dichotomous cultural framework, one may be led to think that the values represented by the two categories are mutually exclusive. Learning in any culture has both an independent (individual) and an interdependent (social) aspect. Human development takes place primarily through social interactions; but the nature of these social interactions varies in large part according to the cultural values of the society within which the child is developing and learning. Thus, independence and interdependence intersect in different ways within the individual, and the way they do is shaped by culture (Raeff, 1997). As we have said, the two categories represent tendencies in emphasis rather than absolute presence or absence of a given value. "Human experience is far too complex to fit neatly into any conceptual scheme. No society is all one thing or another" (Trumbull, Rothstein-Fisch, & Greenfield, 2000, p. 4). There will always be diversity within any group, even if the group members are all recent immigrants from the same state of Mexico.

Another caution has to do with making assumptions about cultures solely on the basis of people's ethnicity or national origin. Other factors are equally, if not more, important. Socioeconomic status (SES) affects tendencies toward individualism or collectivism, with higher SES associated with greater individualism (Hofstede, 2001). Likewise, other aspects of social context, such as whether the family resides in a rural or an urban area, or if the parents have been formally or informally educated, affect the degree to which a family is individualistic or collectivistic. For example, urban life and higher levels of formal education tend to make people more individualistic. In short, oversimplification of culture should be avoided. (See

Greenfield, Keller, Fuligni, & Maynard [2003] for a discussion of the framework's validity.)

THE POTENTIAL OF THE BRIDGING CULTURES FRAMEWORK

Despite the limitations of this framework—and, indeed, any framework is likely to have limitations—it is a good place to start in order to grasp major differences among cultures. Although cultures change over time as they come into contact with each other and as their economic circumstances change, many child-rearing values persist over time (Greenfield, Suzuki, & Rothstein-Fisch, 2006; Hofstede, 1991; Lambert, Hammers, & Frasure-Smith, 1979; Nsamenang & Lamb, 1994). For example, outward acculturation can move people toward individualistic behavior at school or work, but collectivistic values and child-rearing practices are likely to persist at home (Roman, 2006).

The value orientation of collectivism is particularly robust among recent immigrants from rural and poor areas of Mexico and Central and South America, who maintain a strong emphasis on the unity of the family (Delgado-Gaitan, 1994; Valdés, 1996). Thus if the framework proved useful with this population—illuminating dramatic differences between school and home, generating ways to draw on students' strengths, and helping to avoid conflicts in the classroom—then educators could address how it might apply in settings where relations between home and school values were more subtle, such as with second-generation students or in heterogeneous classrooms.

As we seek to build bridges between home and school cultures, we must not reduce complex individuals to simple categories; nevertheless, we cannot ignore the compelling influences of children's home culture on their education. "If we can remember that the framework is just a tool, a heuristic for helping us organize our observations and questions, we can avoid the pitfalls associated with categories" (Trumbull, Rothstein-Fisch, Greenfield, & Quiroz, 2001, p. 4). Taking the perspective that "every child is unique" and treating each student as an individual is, in itself, taking an individualistic perspective, thus negating the strong and powerful influence of culture.

The individualism/collectivism framework has the potential to help educators make implicit cultural patterns explicit. By "naming them and by developing a theoretical understanding of the relationships between the patterns" (Bowers & Flinders, 1990, p. 20), teachers can be supported to understand the kinds of conflicts immigrant students and their families may face. This level of understanding can lead to constructive classroom practices and decisions about management and organization that build upon students' and parents' cultural strengths.

◆ ◆ ◆ ◆ ◆

In Chapter 2, we explore how the group orientation of immigrant Latino students plays out in a variety of classroom situations. We also show how teachers were able to capitalize on students' highly developed social skills to maintain a harmonious instructional environment. In many instances, teachers found that simple solutions to issues of management and organization lay right before their eyes in the cultural strengths of their students.

THE CULTURE OF
THE GROUP

Traditionally, teachers have ignored the notion of peer culture and group norms in the classroom. They have focused their attention on individual learners and have viewed influencing students to behave appropriately as an issue between the teacher and the individual student.

—James Levin and James F. Nolan,
Principles of Classroom Management: A Professional Decision-Making Model

A group orientation is the hallmark of a collectivistic culture. Thus, understanding the depth and meaning of a group orientation is at the heart of teachers' strategies to make classrooms culturally responsive for their students from collectivistic backgrounds. Based on our observations, interviews, and meetings with the teachers, a group orientation, more than anything else, is what distinguishes Bridging Cultures classrooms. According to the Bridging Cultures teachers, it is the concept of "group" that often keeps the learning going and virtually eliminates the need for discipline. Students from collectivistic backgrounds seem to need little or no instruction on how to form groups or function within them. Students' very sense of "self" is constituted by their group membership, with wide-ranging implications for how they think, communicate, learn, and behave (Markus & Kitayama, 1991).

In this chapter we explore the family as the basis for understanding a group orientation and look at what it means to organize classrooms around the idea of the group. We describe idealized versions of two kinds of classroom organization—collectivistic and individualistic. We discuss physical aspects of the classroom and strategies for creating and organizing inclusive groups. We also discuss the nature of group membership through a series of examples on how the group manages itself and cares for its members.

THE FAMILY AS THE BASIS FOR CLASSROOM MANAGEMENT AND ORGANIZATION

The examples throughout this book illustrate a perspective on classroom organization that originates in the family relationships of students from collectivist cultures. Students' behaviors and the beliefs that motivate them emerge from within their families, where group interdependence begins and is most prominent (Delgado-Gaitan, 1994; Markus & Lin, 1999). "In Mexican American cultural contexts, the extended family provides a primary social network for self-definition that affects all relationships beyond the family" (Markus & Lin, 1999, p. 323). Once teachers recognize that the family is the central organizing schema for students' behavior, then they can construct classroom practices that work *with* instead of *against* that orientation (see Gay, 2006). When teachers leverage this knowledge into classroom organization and planning, the benefits are manifest: students engage in more learning because they are not uncomfortably isolated from peers, confused about what counts as appropriate behavior, or fearful of risk taking.

The family notion of working together for the mutual benefit of all is easily applied to group work in schools. Group-oriented classrooms, with students working together *interdependently*, support academic accomplishment and minimize misbehavior. The group is seen as having the potential for self-regulation, cohesiveness, and a synergy that derives from its members acting in concert with each other rather than as individuals.

Others have recognized the metaphor of "the class as a family" as useful for understanding the relationships among immigrant and minority students. For example, Nieto (1999) describes research in a largely Latino high school wherein a teacher's knowledge of the Latino value of *familia* transformed relationships and reversed the trend in dropout rates in that school. However, we question the author's conclusion that students learned to develop collective responsibility for one another through activities such as peer tutoring and mentoring. Those students almost certainly came to school *with* that skill. It may have been ignored, devalued, or even provoked punishment in classrooms where helping others and supporting group efforts were seen as either unrelated to academic achievement or, worse, as the sources of classroom disruption. However, once collective responsibility was valued, it could apparently reemerge.

In a prominent book on elementary classroom management, the authors present four teachers as successful, but different, exemplary classroom managers (Weinstein & Mignano, 2003). One teacher, Viviana Love, is an immigrant herself, from rural Puerto Rico. She structures her 1st grade bilingual class as she would a family, telling parents, "At home *you're* the parents . . . but at school, *I'm* the mother. We're all family, one big family, all Hispanics, and we all help each other" (p. 15). Her comment echoes the proverb "*La maestra es la segunda madre*" ("The teacher is the second mother").

Thus, even without precise and explicit explanations of why the family metaphor is so fundamental to student success and well-managed classrooms, insightful teachers recognize its usefulness. Yet without a theoretical framework to guide teachers' classroom organization, such intuitive knowledge can go untapped or be only partially effective. A limited understanding of how critical "groupness" is for collectivistic students can result in mixed messages unless teachers make explicit rules about when to help others and when to work alone. Both individual work and group work are important, but until teachers recognize the cultural strengths that students bring to schools, they may fail to fully use those strengths to the benefit of students' success in school.

INDIVIDUALISM AND COLLECTIVISM: TWO APPROACHES TO CLASSROOM ORGANIZATION

Knowledge of the collectivistic cultural value of "groupness" has become the foundation for many of the innovations of the Bridging Cultures teachers. However, the individual is not absent in the collectivistic orientation to the classroom. The individual remains an active entity but is not the primary focus for organization and management. If a group activity does not work well, or if a student has certain special needs, the teacher can certainly respond with appropriate actions. Incorporating the needs of individual students is not meant to represent the "last resort" when organizing classrooms. In reality, the processes of developing group activities and coming to know the individual students happen simultaneously. However, the group model reflects special emphasis on collectivistic values and, in particular, the values of the family.

In the individualistic classroom, knowledge of individuals is the basis for classroom management (see McCaslin et al., 2006; Robinson & Ricord Gresiemer, 2006). The emphasis is on supressing each student's potential for distracting, disrupting, or disrespectful behaviors. Theoretically, when each student must be considered as a single unit, classroom management should become more complex. In an individually oriented classroom, even when students are grouped, the teacher is likely to see them as a collection of individuals who are potentially in competition with each other (Isaac, 1999). Or, as a new teacher told one of us, "I never realized that 30 students equal 60 arms moving all at once!" In a classroom oriented toward an individualistic approach, families are part of the management equation, but primarily when problem behaviors escalate to the point where teachers feel they need support from the home (Evertson, Emmer, & Worsham, 2006).

Figure 2.1 compares an idealized version of two approaches to classroom organization: one collectivistic and the other individualistic. In the collectivistic organization shown in the top triangle, the teacher begins with an understanding of the family (as indicated by the arrows under the triangle). This understanding guides classroom

FIGURE 2.1

Collectivistic and Individualistic Classroom Organization

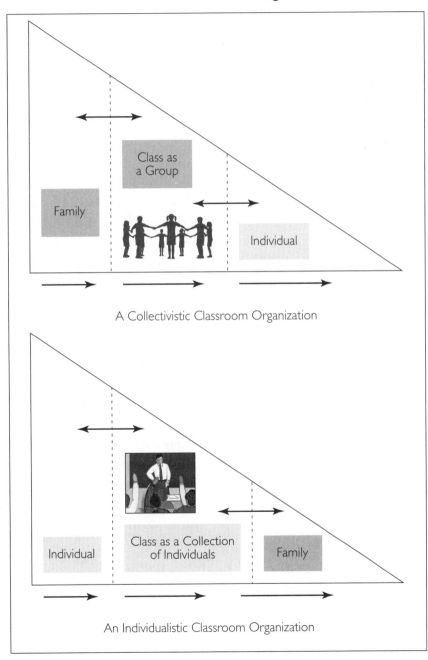

A Collectivistic Classroom Organization

An Individualistic Classroom Organization

management strategies that focus on the class as a group, much like the family as a unit. A dashed line and a double arrow indicate that the flow of information goes back and forth between the classroom and the family. The class is depicted as one group in which all the learners are linked with each other and the teacher as a whole. Individual students are factored into a collectivistic classroom, though not as a starting point. Teachers in collectivistic classrooms incorporate their knowledge of individuals into organizational practices, as indicated by another dashed line and double arrow. But the placement of "Family" and "Class as a Group" at the wider end of the triangle indicates that the majority of classroom practices are based on the group rather than a loose confederation of individuals.

The lower triangle in Figure 2.1 shows an individualistic classroom organization, which begins with an emphasis on the individuals in the class. Teachers in this kind of classroom might try to promote the values of independence, choice, and individual decision making to promote self-reliance, self-respect, and self-esteem. The emphasis is clearly on each child's individual needs. Thus the class is seen as a collection of individuals, each requiring something (or, more likely, some *things*) different. The students in the figure are sitting at individual desks, poised to show what each one knows—depicting the values of individual achievement and self-expression. Students in such a classroom would not necessarily be enlisted to help or support others. Because classroom organization is based on the individual, "Individual" and "Class as a Collection of Individuals" occupy the wider end of the triangle. But, as in the collectivistic model, the family does have a role, though the teacher may think of it as an afterthought or use it as a focus of punishment, revealed in a threat such as, "Do I need to call your parent?"

RECONSIDERING CONVENTIONAL WISDOM ON GROUP ORGANIZATION AND SUPPORT

Research has identified a number of strategies that promote the effectiveness of cooperative groups. Such strategies include teachers modeling how to work in groups in order to promote interdependence along with individual responsibility within a group. For example, teachers may model how students should give and receive help from other students. Group skills such as these are well honed by the immigrant Latino students we have observed. However, unless teachers are aware of students' group-related skills, these may be overlooked or undermined, or—worst of all—students may be punished for using them.

A well-meaning individualistic teacher with collectivistic students may instruct students to "take a vote" to resolve a conflict in a group situation, when in fact this strategy might *cause* conflict when it clashes with a preexisting orientation toward developing consensus to resolve disagreement. Girard and Koch (1996) say that a consensus

> reflects a considered agreement that everyone involved—unanimously—accepts a specific course of action as best for the group and agrees to support it regardless of private preferences and interests. Consensus encourages a deeper level of conflict analysis and encourages all participants in the negotiation to express their opinions and concerns. (p. 87)

The following vignette illustrates how important consensus can be for students socialized in collectivistic homes.

THE HAUNTING HALLOWEEN

The students in Mrs. Pérez's 5th grade class were faced with a difficult choice: should they have their own Halloween party in class, wear costumes, and bring refreshments from home to share with each other, or should they don their costumes and go to a communitywide parade and celebration at the neighboring naval base? Some wanted to stay in the classroom for a private party, but more were drawn to the community celebration. Mrs. Pérez decided to have the children vote. The class would then do what the majority wanted.

As it happened, most voted to go to the parade; only six voted to stay at school, two of whom eventually came around to thinking the parade was a good idea. But four children did not want to go to the parade and continued to feel disappointed about not having the class party. Suspecting that they were not comfortable going to the large event with so many people, Mrs. Pérez gave them the option of staying behind with a parent helper. Only one child, Selena, chose this option. The others ultimately went to the parade. As it turned out, Selena stayed home that day. At the celebration, Selena's classmates missed her immensely and found it impossible to enjoy themselves.

Troubled feelings about the incident did not fade quickly. Weeks went by and Mrs. Pérez continued to hear small but persistent conversations about how sad it was that Selena hadn't gotten to do what she wanted. The class seemed unsettled about the outcome of their decision-making process. It wasn't until Mrs. Pérez participated in the Bridging Cultures Project that she understood how the children's reaction might be related to the values of the children's collectivistic culture. Her students were reflecting a deep-seated discomfort with a process that inherently separates members from the group. Mrs. Pérez realized that a more extended process could have led to a full-group consensus and avoided the turmoil that ensued. (Adapted from Trumbull, Rothstein-Fisch, & Greenfield, 2000. Reprinted with permission from WestEd. All rights reserved.)

In the past, Bridging Cultures teachers may have intuitively understood their students' "groupness," but it was access to the individualism/collectivism framework that crystallized a conscious awareness of this orientation. When we asked Mr. Mercado which practices inspired by Bridging Cultures he used most with his 4th graders, he responded,

Collaborative ones, because they are natural. They seem to go with the flow. I think of the example of perming straight hair. I leave it as it is; I am not going against the grain. [The class] runs more smoothly. It promotes more harmony and a much more finished product.

Mr. Mercado emphasizes collaborative learning "because the students can produce more and are more engaged in the learning process." Failing to capitalize on students' culture-based strengths does not result in simply a lost opportunity; it undercuts the cultural values of the family and can cause students to feel torn between the behaviors valued at home and those valued at school.

THE POWER AND RESPONSIBILITY OF THE GROUP

From the beginning of the school year, Mrs. Pérez talks explicitly with her students about the "power of the group." From the start, her students know that their actions are important to the rest of the class, and this orientation is evident throughout the day in virtually every learning experience. The power of the group comes through in students' harmonious and supportive peer relationships, their respect for each other and for adults, and their striving for group success.

We have observed firsthand what happens when these qualities are allowed to flourish. They support the smooth operation of the class and maximize learning opportunities, in part because students help each other learn and also because little time is diverted from meaningful learning to classroom management issues.

Ms. Daley expects her 2nd grade students to rely on each other whenever possible. "I can give an assignment to a group and walk away," she said. "On a rare occasion, a child will ask me how to do something. [I say] 'I think I know who you have to go to first.' Then they find someone to ask. Now they do it on their own." She reported that "even the most hard-to-discipline children are willing to listen to their peers. . . . It is an expectation within the community."

The following example from Mrs. Hernandez's combined classroom of kindergartners, 1st graders, and 2nd graders shows how the kinds of behaviors demonstrated in Bridging Cultures classrooms also result in a sense of responsibility among the students.

DINA LEADS ALPHABET PRACTICE

Mrs. Hernandez's 18 students are working together on the rug practicing alphabet skills. She has to leave the group to work with a parent volunteer (the father of one of the students), who is building some shelving for the classroom. She asks Dina, a 1st grader, to supervise the practice. Although Mrs. Hernandez is away from the circle-time activity, Dina continues to move the group through the routine. She climbs on a chair, points to each letter of the alphabet with her pointer, and has the children chorally say each letter.

The children stay very focused, with no off-task behavior. Mrs. Hernandez returns to the group after about 10 minutes, and she and Dina continue to lead the group in alphabet-related activities. Ultimately, there are no disruptions for nearly 45 minutes of rug time. The children sit very close to each other, but there are no confrontations or problems. The children appear to be very attentive to the activities.

We posit that because classroom organization and management were designed with collectivistic students in mind, no disciplinary problems arose. Mrs. Hernandez's expectations were in line with how the students had been socialized at home: to work together in harmony for the good of the group. The rituals of student-led morning songs, alphabet practice, and calendar activities prevalent in this classroom evoked helpfulness from others. Corrections by students about their peers' performance did not appear to embarrass, discredit, or humiliate them. Instead, such corrections appeared to be consistently accepted as a way to support others' learning. "They would help a friend—not to shame them," Mrs. Hernandez explained, "but they'd move the pointer to the correct word. Never— ever—to tease; just to help."

The next observation comes from Ms. Daley's 2nd grade classroom.

TAKING MS. DALEY'S PLACE

Ms. Daley is about to read *La Calle Es Libre (The Street Is Free)*, when the children inform her that they already know the book. "Could you tell the story?" she asks. While Ms. Daley fills out a required health document, six children line up in front of the rest of the class. Each child tells a part of the story. One girl walks around and shows the pictures in the book to the rest of the class. Other children who are part of the group in front of the class correct or amend the story as needed. The seated children in the audience seem genuinely content to be observer-learners rather than the leader-participants.

This observation is interesting from several perspectives: (1) young students (2nd graders) quickly responded to a teacher's request to carry out an academic activity without her guidance, showing a high level of self-management and group organization and support; (2) the leaders were self-selected and apparently accepted by the group without any squabbling or discussion; (3) classmates pitched in to help for the good of the whole just as those who were in the audience were helping to keep the group functioning optimally; and (4) the self-appointed leaders worked collaboratively and without any strife. The teacher did not need to waste students' time by asking them to sit quietly until she could teach, and she was able to take care of an important task without interruption while the children continued to learn.

PHYSICAL ORGANIZATION OF GROUP-ORIENTED CLASSROOMS

The group orientation of Bridging Cultures classrooms is reflected in their physical organization. One of the first and most important requirements for group work is the appropriate room arrangement (Evertson, Emmer, & Worsham, 2006). The Bridging Cultures teachers have created learning environments that accommodate group work and diminish the need for behavioral control from the teacher.

Desk Arrangements, Rug Time, and Physical Proximity

In five of the seven Bridging Cultures classrooms, desks are arranged in clusters of four, with children facing each other. The two exceptions are in the classes of the youngest children (kindergarten through 2nd grade), where a large rug dominates the room, surrounded by learning centers for three or four children each. In all cases, teachers have overtly group-oriented classrooms. At any given time, the children are either all together on the large rug, or they are in small groups.

Rug time is especially common in Bridging Cultures classrooms and differs somewhat from what might be typical in other classrooms. In most elementary school classrooms, teachers require children to identify and maintain their own spaces, using such strategies as individual carpet squares to help children identify "their" area on the rug or a grid to demarcate one square for each child. In contrast, Bridging Cultures teachers do not prevent children from having the physical closeness to each other that they seem to seek. The concept of owning space, if only temporarily, is probably foreign to these students. Especially noticeable in the classrooms of Mrs. Hernandez, Ms. Daley, and Mrs. Pérez, children sat close together on the rug, often shoulder to shoulder, or occasionally touching each other's hair. Contrary to what many teachers might expect, this kind of behavior never became disruptive. Instead, it seemed to sustain the children's focus, as if they were getting some comfort from contact with their friends.

When asked during a debriefing about the children's physical proximity to the teacher and to each other during circle time, Mrs. Pérez said the proximity brings the children closer together as a social group. Thus the nearness of the students to each other is another reminder of how the group stays together. The closeness never appeared to lead to any conflict or altercation, and it didn't seem to distract the children from the learning activity. Rather, it seemed desirable and sought out by the students. This practice may not work for all students, but on no occasion did we observe any problems caused by physical contact in Bridging Cultures classrooms.

The culturally collectivistic students in these classrooms seem to understand the need for the whole group to participate in rug time. In Mrs. Hernandez's K–1–2 class, children helped their friends get to the circle promptly, were attentive to the needs of the whole group, and seemed to demonstrate group pride in their accomplishment of getting the whole group altogether. Group activities proceeded with no disruptions for periods lasting up to one hour! An understanding of this tendency to seek physical proximity could lead teachers to eliminate or modify the rule that tells students "Keep your hands to yourself." At times, it may be helpful to hold hands or touch some- one nearby in appropriate ways, as we observed. Therefore, before establishing fixed classroom rules, teachers should consider what the children do naturally according to their own cultural models and within appropriate boundaries (Carlson, 2006).

Bulletin Boards and Walls

Teachers in Bridging Cultures classrooms use bulletin boards and walls for a range of purposes, such as exhibiting student work, post- ing rules or directions for tasks (for example, the steps in the writ- ing process), motivating students through inspirational posters, or sharing personal facts about "students of the week." Bulletin boards and walls are notable for their reflection of both the academic and the personal lives of students. Some sections may be devoted to stu- dent writing or to charts and illustrations from various projects, while other sections display photographs and drawings of families. Bulletin boards in Bridging Cultures classrooms often reflect a collectivistic orientation not only in content but also in the way they are created— frequently by the whole group.

Mr. Mercado's classroom of 4th and 5th grade students (who are in their first year of an English-only curriculum) provides an excellent example of the use of bulletin boards.

MR. MERCADO'S BULLETIN BOARDS

A prominent bulletin board, titled "Tell Us About Your Grandmother," displays children's neatly crafted papers (with their earlier drafts underneath). The showcased papers are a result of children's fascination with their grandmothers, who often still reside in the country of origin, such as Mexico or El Salvador. According to Mr. Mercado, the children all wanted to share information about their grandmothers, but they needed a fixed structure. He allowed them to construct a framework of questions as a way to systematically prepare their descriptive paragraphs according to state standards. The children decided to ask questions about where their grandmother lived, how old she was, what foods she cooked, what they like to do with their grandmother, and how much they loved their grandmothers.

During one class period, Mr. Mercado draws the children's attention back to the bulletin board, asking the students to remember what they did to describe their own grandmothers as a way to link the academic skill of descriptive writing about a family member to a new topic—descriptive poetry. But even then, the centrality of family is evident when Mr. Mercado asks Yasmin, "Why do people write poems?" and she replies, "I'd give my mother a poem to tell her I love her."

Mr. Mercado's classroom also includes several large laminated charts on punctuation, proofreading marks, and cognates in Spanish and English (i.e., words coming from the same Latin roots in both English and Spanish). These commercially produced charts hang above the chalkboard—higher than the eye-level display about grandmothers. In this way, grandmothers are always present in the room at the children's level, but the information that the children need for editing is still in plain view.

Murals, a common sight in Mexico, appear on the interior and exterior walls of many schools in Southern California. Bridging Cultures schools are no exception. One large-scale group mural project was initiated with help from a UCLA art student volunteering in Mr. Mercado's class. The goal was to understand more about the community—Venice Beach, California. The project began with a neighborhood walk to identify points of interest, and upon their return to the classroom, the students decided what they wanted to contribute to a large mural that was intended for the hallway to share with others. A student who had difficulty drawing was happy to paint the background or help fill in colors where others had produced outlines. In this way, everyone contributed and felt pride in accomplishing something together.

Similarly, Ms. Altchech's 5th graders had painted a large mural, "The Animals of the Wetlands," that hung in a prominent spot in the classroom. All students collaborated on the mural, but they could choose how they wanted to contribute—by painting an individual element, such as a bird; by contributing to a team-constructed element, such as a grassy area or a flock of birds; or as a general artist working on the background or assembling the separate sections of the mural. To Ms. Altchech, the range of choices about how to participate made good sense, because by 5th grade, even students from highly collectivistic families are likely to have absorbed a degree of individualism. Some may, in fact, prefer to work alone. The result was that all students could look at the mural with pride on the basis of their contributions to the whole.

Approximating the Home Environment

Two other examples of the physical classroom environment are notable because they demonstrate how the classroom may resemble the home environment. The first, Mrs. Eyler's kindergarten classroom, has limited space, equipment, and materials. Three teachers share the classroom simultaneously. However, this situation is not entirely undesirable. The children come to school and see their teachers sharing a common space and resources—a situation that is similar to what they experience at home, with everyone working together in close proximity. The children do not seem hampered by the lack of open space.

The second example is Mrs. Pérez's classroom desk. It represents a similar, smaller-scale crossover of home and school. Her desktop displays three photos: one of Mrs. Pérez's family and two of the entire class. By displaying the personal family photo, Mrs. Pérez brings *her* family into the classroom. According to Mrs. Pérez, the students ask questions about her husband (also an elementary school teacher) and her two sons as a way of connecting to the teacher—establishing and maintaining a personal relationship. The two photos of her students are prominently displayed as well. How esteemed the students must feel to have their photos alongside that of Mrs. Pérez's family!

ESTABLISHING AND ORGANIZING INCLUSIVE GROUPS

All seven of the teachers reported using cooperative group work before they received the Bridging Cultures training, but the amount of time devoted to it has changed, as has the quality of it. With a greater understanding of the children's home values, the teachers have a deeper sense of why group work has always tended to be successful. As a result, they have increased their use of both small and large groups.

Many of the examples in this section are drawn from the 2nd grade classroom of Mrs. Pérez with good reason. The vast majority of Mrs. Pérez's students are children of farm workers. They live in a rural area that is surrounded by large areas of strawberry fields and lemon groves. This area is less urban than that of the other Bridging Cultures teachers. Living in an agricultural area with family members engaged in farm work (and earning low wages) is more likely to be associated with collectivistic values (Hofstede, 2001).

To encourage her class to function as a whole unit, Mrs. Pérez and her students recite their own group pledge in addition to the daily pledge to the flag. This second pledge illustrates how the individual can contribute to the well-being of the whole—in this case, the world:

> I pledge allegiance to the world,
> To cherish every living thing,
> To care for earth and sea and air,
> With peace and freedom everywhere.

Mrs. Pérez says, "[Coming together as a group] sets the tone in the morning. We say the pledge together and look into each other's eyes and connect. When they are in a circle together, they look at each other at the beginning and end of the day and everything else is connected that way." The class ends the day by sharing their thoughts on the best things that happened that day. Mrs. Pérez reported that the children always talk about group experiences. "Nothing is ever said about them standing out by themselves," she said. "It is always something that *we* did."

Mrs. Pérez's class is organized around a set of activity areas through which children rotate. By organizing the children in groups of two or more students, Mrs. Pérez ensures that children are working with or very close to others. In fact, in none of our observations in her classroom did we see children working alone. The room is organized with a set number of chairs at each of the learning centers: six at the reading comprehension table; four at a learning center activity table; and two each at an art table, where children work on a theme-related project; a games/books/library center; a computer technology center; a listening center; and a "transition corner," where students read posters on a wall display and look at books jointly created by the whole class. Each station has instructions about task goals and methods, and perhaps partly because of that, we never observed any conflicts as students moved efficiently to each station and immediately began the task.

Mrs. Pérez also uses a simple numbering system to organize the class as well as to encourage student participation. The students have a number that establishes them as a member of a particular group.

Mrs. Pérez calls upon students by groups, and she reports that they are much more likely to volunteer as a result. "Although they do go up alone, they feel like they are a part of a group," she said. "I have wasted so much time [in the past] deciding the order [to call upon students]. This way it is spontaneous, and the children look at each other to encourage each other—they face each other." Mrs. Pérez said that it is surprising to see that sometimes "the quiet, shy people will be part of the first group." Students can pass if they do not want to respond, but, Mrs. Pérez reported, students eventually do respond "because they are part of a group—resulting in 100 percent [participation] time and time again."

Mrs. Pérez also reported that the best way to get something accomplished is to bring the children together in their group circle. "We begin our day in a class circle," she said, "and we end our class in a circle."

RISK TAKING IN THE GROUP CONTEXT

Early in the Bridging Cultures project, as she was experimenting with groups, Mrs. Pérez reflected on how the group orientation of the classroom affects the students' risk taking: "Togetherness releases the stress, and they are more willing to risk. They feel more confident. I'm still struggling with how to [do it]. But we [are a] team." Reducing stress while increasing the willingness to take risks is critical for optimal learning (see Doyle, 2006). Group work also reduces the need for heavy-handed classroom management: if students are not anxious about their work or assignments, they can concentrate on learning. This effect is particularly true if they are newcomers to the culture or if they are English language learners.

Mrs. Pérez's comments in a later interview provide additional observations about the children's willingness to take risks in a group-oriented classroom. She noted the presence of "way more risk taking—and that is in spite of more shy children this year. . . . But yet they risk because they are comfortable." Citing an example, she said that working on a poem together yielded "100 percent participation.

Before that . . . I might have a few children go up and say a poem or take turns at the microphone. [It was] much more individualistic. It is so much more powerful when they are all together, doing the same things." Mrs. Pérez reported that if one of the students has not participated, the children will say, "Juan hasn't read his! [They] ask Juan to do it too. The children . . . want each person to present." The students in Mrs. Pérez's class monitor each other to ensure that everyone in the group participates. Thus the group encourages full participation and offers support in ways that are culturally harmonious.

ADULTS AS MEMBERS OF THE GROUP

Group inclusiveness embraces both children and adults. Bridging Cultures teachers were generally included as a part of group activities, though, as we have seen, the group will continue even if the teachers leave for a short time. The teachers often took the role of facilitator, to keep activities on track. Teachers have reported, and we have observed, that the children ask for their participation in a wide range of contexts—at rug time, during discussions, or at lunchtime.

Even observers were made to feel part of the class—a testament to the students' strong orientation to include people in their group. For example, throughout our observations, the students monitored what we were doing, always smiling, as if to say, "We want you to feel part of our group." The experience was completely different from the more typical situation in which observers become a distraction, diverting attention from the lesson to something novel. The children never seemed to disconnect from their learning activities, but instead would glance over as if to be sure we were connecting to the social setting.

For example, Mrs. Hernandez's class was quick to notice that the observers couldn't see the pictures in the book during the reading of *100 Hungry Ants*. A student named Celeste asked the teacher, "Why aren't you showing the pictures to the teachers?" in reference to not sharing the pictures with the observers. This orientation is particularly interesting given the young age of the students, who were primarily kindergartners and 1st graders (with a few 2nd graders as well). The ability to take the "outlook of another" reminds us of the Piagetian task of "the three mountains" as a test of egocentrism: the mountain task requires children to describe what others are seeing from an opposing viewpoint. These children seemed to understand this even in kindergarten (Piaget, 1952).

In Mr. Mercado's classroom, guests were overtly included. At the start of one observation, Mr. Mercado began by saying, "This is my friend, Dr. Rothstein-Fisch." He wrote the long and complicated name on the chalkboard, and the class said in chorus, "Good morning, Dr. Rothstein-Fisch." During the two-hour visit, the teacher made several references to the observer: "Let's show Dr. Rothstein-Fisch what we know about . . ." "Janet, tell Dr. Rothstein-Fisch how you are spelling that word so she will know." "Dr. Rothstein-Fisch hasn't been in our class while we've been reading our book. I told her about the book, but how can she find out about it?" The children responded with a list of ideas: (1) read it to her; (2) let her borrow the book; (3) have her see the movie; (4) write to her about it; (5) explain it to her; (6) tell her the most significant part.

Mr. Mercado had planned a review of the book the class was reading, *Annie and the Old One*, that day, but he set up the context for doing that task with a larger, inclusive social purpose. To "help the observer understand" and ultimately make her part of the group, students in each group organized to tell a portion of the story. The students decided collectively how the observer would best under-stand the story, and then each group told a part of the story to the classroom observer in chronological order. Not only was this strat-egy a natural approach for the students, it also mirrored the kind of language arts instruction known to promote reading comprehension (Pearson & Duke, 2002). To make judgments about what an outsider would need to know about the story for it to make sense, students had to consider what they knew and determine how to express it best to someone else.

In a similar fashion, Mr. Mercado encouraged his students to con-nect personally with his classroom volunteer, Mr. G., a retired member of the community. During math instruction, Mr. Mercado asked the children, "Who uses geometry?" The children responded by saying, "architects," "abstract artists," "*carpinteros*" (carpenters). "Mr. G.'s son is a carpenter," said Mr. Mercado. "What does he do? Let's say the door is a little bit too big, what would happen?" Responding together, the children said, "It wouldn't close." Bringing Mr. G's son and his occupation into the discussion was a natural approach in this classroom of mostly immigrant Latino students, for whom family is more important than anything else. This example acknowledged the importance of Mr. G.'s family while linking its significance to a math concept.

GROUP REGULATION OF BEHAVIOR AND CONFLICT

Many of our observations revealed a substantial amount of student leadership. Earlier in the chapter we described instances of students taking charge when the teacher's attention was required elsewhere. In the case of Ms. Daley's class, students just pitched in for the good of the group, whether as leaders or as listeners. The same was true in Mrs. Hernandez's class, where the appointed leader took charge without any disruption to the ongoing lesson. In both instances, a deep and well-established mutual understanding about behavior and learning was established between the teacher and the students. In these classrooms, everyone seemed to know that group learning was expected.

Examples of student-led practices covered a wide range of activities, including correcting a sentence riddled with errors as part of a Daily Oral Language lesson; leading the morning calendar, weather, alphabet, and song routine; guiding fellow students in a lesson on math facts; and maintaining social order in the absence of the teacher. It's difficult to know the extent to which these practices resulted from the Bridging Cultures Project. Teachers may have been influenced by previous exposure to critical pedagogy (Freire, 1970, as described by Mrs. Pérez), other philosophies, or professional development on collaborative learning groups and leadership. (Mr. Mercado and Ms. Daley became National Board certified teachers during the five years of the project.) However, it is clear that students readily took on a variety of leadership roles and that their classrooms operated without disruptions or conflicts. Evidence points to students' collectivistic socialization at home as at least one significant source of the social skills they exhibited.

For collectivistic students, leadership appears to come from the desire to contribute to the group rather than to gain individual recognition. Classroom goals are met when student leaders use their desire and skills to ensure that the group is on task and participating in appropriate ways. During our many hours of observation, the student leaders (who, teachers reported, shared leadership across tasks and days) were highly effective in managing their peers, alleviating the need for teacher intervention.

Class Meetings

During one observation toward the end of the school year, when Mrs. Pérez was teaching 5th grade, a regular Friday class meeting was taking place. The class president gathered ideas about what topics should be included in the meeting. The class president and vice president conducted the entire meeting as the teacher listened from the back of the room. The first topic of discussion was elections for new class officers. There was a great deal of discussion about who had been elected previously and who had not, with concerns expressed about how those children not elected would feel and what they would think. At one point a student said, "Tony won't be nominated because he's too American."

This seemed like a moment that would prompt immediate teacher intervention, but Mrs. Pérez honored the group's process and remained silent as she watched. After a few seconds, the children articulated their concern about this potentially hurtful remark. They discussed how that might make Tony feel, and they suggested telling Tony how to gain the good graces of the group: he should be less aloof in discussing his high grades and participation in special gifted classes. In this case, Tony was not ultimately nominated as a class leader, but the students agreed that he would be considered a top contender for the next election. In a sense, the children were telling Tony not to "stick out" and be boastful, so as to draw him back to group acceptance.

Tony appeared to be European American and likely had an individualistic cultural perspective that led him to seek to improve his self-esteem by emphasizing his individual achievement and his cognitive intelligence. In contrast, his classmates were trying to incorporate him into the group and help him to understand the need to fit in without grandstanding. This observation demonstrates the real power of a well-functioning group—to have everyone included. Students from collectivistic backgrounds did not want to belittle the accomplishments of a student who might be in honors classes, but they recommended that he not brag about it because that would make him stand out from the whole and make him less a part of the group. The class suggested ways for Tony to become part of the group again, and possibly a class leader in the future.

The power of the group is only as mighty as the teacher allows. In the situation with Tony, the teacher held back, waiting to see what would happen, but she later reported that she knew the group well enough to trust them to "do the right thing," and she had to provide enough time to allow that to emerge. By respecting the group, she helped empower the students with their own problem-solving skills. We may imagine what the outcome might have been had the teacher stepped in: punishment for the initial remark about Tony or digression into a discussion of what it means to be "an American." In either case, these classroom management decisions would have shifted the focus to the teacher to solve the problem without allowing the demonstration of the natural abilities of the students to find a culturally harmonious solution to student conflict.

This example also relates to an important aspect of the collectivistic value of the group: fitting in or standing out. Standing out from the group may be something immigrant Latino parents strive to avoid for their children. Quiroz and Greenfield (1996) report the experience of a Mexican immigrant mother when her daughter's teacher told her that her child was outstanding. "I did not know what to do about her being 'outstanding.' I had tried to show my daughter not to 'show off' or to be cruel to others, but it seemed that it was not working" (p. 6). The mother may have understood the word *outstanding* to mean literally "standing out" from the group, something highly undesirable in a family with a collectivistic orientation. The mother's fear that her daughter would draw attention to herself, at the risk of being different from other students, must be understood in the context of a group orientation: in fact, the mother was socializing her daughter *not* to stand out from the rest of the class.

The Group as Manager

During our observations, we saw many instances in which the group took responsibility for classroom behavior. The following examples illustrate the managerial role the group maintains for itself.

During an outdoor activity, two 2nd grade classes combined to form one large group. Groups lined up and went to eight different "stations" featuring different activities, such as jump rope, monkey bars, zig-zag jumping, four-square, hot potato, and long jump. When a child arrived late, Ms. Daley said, "You've never been at that station? Ask your group what to do." Her directive underscored the responsibility of the group to help the late-arriving student, thereby eliminating the teacher's need to explain directions again.

In a second example, during a long storytelling episode, one student began relating to the story of *The River* by sharing his knowledge of the subject. He spoke for some time, and a few children began to whisper to each other or engage in subdued chatter during the discussion. Nearby children said, "Shhhh," and immediately the whispering children complied and redirected themselves to listening. This incident was especially impressive because these were kindergarten and 1st grade children. They had already been sitting for a long while, but their willingness to be regulated by peers attests to their wanting to be part of the whole. This minor incident was not even noticed by other members of the group, nor did the teacher, Mrs. Hernandez, indicate that she had observed it.

Group awareness also helped Mrs. Eyler solve a mystery. She was distributing pictures collected from the previous days to the students who had created them. When she discovered one with writing that could not be deciphered, she asked the small group nearby, "Who writes like this?" The children knew immediately that it belonged to one particular child.

During an observation in Ms. Altchech's class, a child had just returned from a lengthy absence due to a court order involving child abuse. The whole class was genuinely glad to see her, and yet they carried on as if she had never left, not making her feel apart from them, but rather instantly included. Some time later, several students were dismissed for chorus. A classmate came back hurriedly into the class because she remembered that her returning classmate might still like to be in chorus.

But what happens when group consciousness appears to cross the line and students run the risk of embarrassing a fellow classmate? In one example, Ms. Daley's 2nd grade class was on the playground, and many students were playing on the monkey bars. A boy, apparently anxious for his turn, told the others, "She's losing!" But a girl also waiting for her turn retorted, "No, she's *learning*."

It is difficult to know whether the comment "she's losing" emerged from the boy's annoyance that the student on the climbing apparatus was taking too long to cross, which appeared to be the case. However, the second student's comment, "She's learning," seems to be an effort to quash the boy's criticism and to encourage her classmate. From a collectivistic perspective, she was bringing both of her classmates back into the group. The boy's comments were rebuffed to draw him back into the group, and the struggling girl's efforts were supported as a way for her to gain inclusion into the group of those who could successfully cross the monkey bars. When asked about this scenario, Ms. Daley said that the children now celebrate each other's accomplishments, whereas in years past they didn't do that. Now she feels as though she can create more of a "family" feeling in the class. She can also teach them by reminding them, "You know how you feel when someone accomplishes something in your family . . . We do that at school."

GROUP CONTINGENCIES

In setting up groups, it is important to consider what is truly rewarding for students. When teachers set up interdependent group contingencies—requiring the entire group to reach a designated goal—several advantages follow, according to Robinson and Ricord Greisemer (2006):

> Interdependent group contingencies have several advantages that make them appealing to teachers. First, interdependent group contingencies have been found to be time-efficient, cost-effective, and easy to implement. Either all or none of the students meet the goal and receive reinforcement, making it less complicated procedurally while allowing more activities to become available for reinforcement (e.g., field trips, extra recess, and pizza parties). Second, because individual students are not directly singled out (even though there may be a target student in mind), there is little risk of individual students being targeted for ridicule based on their performance. Finally, because it is in everyone's best interest to meet the goals, cooperation and encouragement are more likely to occur. (p. 796)

We agree that groups do help students to work cooperatively, but the notion that this is contingency-based because of external reinforcement should be reexamined in light of cultural values. In general, considerable research suggests that the whole notion of external reinforcement should be reconsidered (see, for example, Deci, Koestner, & Ryan, 2001). Students from collectivistic homes do not get rewarded for working well together; they are expected to do so without an extrinsic reward. The contingencies that are most powerful are social ones, based on relationships. It is likely that, for these students, working together is already an intrinsic reward.

◆ ◆ ◆ ◆ ◆

In this chapter we have offered a wide range of examples demonstrating how the culture of the group operates in the classroom. We saw how students contributed to managing activities and disturbances themselves. This kind of monitoring assists learning because teachers are not distracted by students committing minor infractions. The children, even those as young as kindergarten age, can help maintain a proper learning environment. As a result of the group's efforts, more time is spent engaged in learning, and very little is taken up with reprimands, rebuffs, redirections, or rejections.

In the next chapter, we look at families as the first and most logical place to understand "where students are coming from" and how this can affect classroom functioning.

FAMILIES: RESOURCES FOR ORGANIZATION AND MANAGEMENT

It appears . . . that teachers and parents can use similar mechanisms to influence student behavior; however, the nature of their contributions is different . . . [P]arents' involvement often focuses on socialization for culture and school rather than instruction whereas teachers focus more on instruction and socialization at school. These two roles represent different but essential resources for children's development.

—Joan M. T. Walker and Kathleen V. Hoover-Dempsey,
"Why Research on Parental Involvement Is Important to Classroom
Management" in *Handbook of Classroom Management*

Families set the context for children's cognitive and social development. They establish the foundation for children's orientation to the classroom in terms of their patterns for relating to peers and adults and how they approach learning tasks (Walker & Hoover-Dempsey, 2006). For these reasons, it is crucially important for teachers to form partnerships with families and find ways to promote two-way, transactional learning, with parents learning from the teacher about school expectations and teachers learning from parents about children's socialization at home over time.

In this chapter, we investigate the relationships among cultural values, family involvement in schooling, and teachers' approaches to classroom organization and management. This "up-front" discussion about the role of families in classroom management follows from our discussion in Chapter 2 indicating that families factor in at the *beginning* of the management equation.

We use the terms *parents* and *families* interchangeably because not all children are cared for by their parents, yet parents are most frequently children's primary source of socialization and are responsible for their attendance and, to varying degrees, their success in school. However, in some cases the responsible individuals for any given student could be grandparents or other relatives. We also like the term *family* because students are often taught important behavioral skills from older siblings or cousins, particularly how to work in groups, how to give and receive help, and the consequences of *not* being part of the group.

CHALLENGES TO CROSS-CULTURAL UNDERSTANDING BETWEEN SCHOOLS AND FAMILIES

Perhaps one of the greatest challenges to cross-cultural understanding between schools and families arises from the all-too-natural human instinct to judge differences in approaches to child development and education as unenlightened or simply wrong (Valencia & Solórzano, 1997). And when one person or group (such as the professionals from the dominant culture) holds more social power than the other (the family members from a nondominant culture), it is not hard to figure out whose judgment will hold more sway (Harry, Allen, & McLaughlin, 1995; Lipka, 1998; Salas, 2004).

When teachers attribute students' "inappropriate" behavior to cultural deficits in child rearing, they may consciously exclude parents from the problem-solving process. (We put the term *inappropriate* in quotation marks because judgments about appropriateness are relative to one's cultural perspective. What is considered "too quiet" or "too noisy," for instance, is extremely variable according to culture.) In some cases, parents are contacted only "when it is apparent that the teacher and school have explored all the interventions at their disposal" (Levin & Nolan, 2007, p. 243). In other words, the school staff members wait until they are desperate rather than at the apparent onset of the problem, when information from the family could possibly prevent further stress for all concerned.

Blaming parents for students' failure to behave in expected ways can seriously corrupt the essential relationship between the teacher and the family. Such a deficit approach to difference is not only ill informed, it prevents teachers from gaining the kind of information that might very well help students reach their full potential. Research makes it clear that teachers who reach out to families and are open to learning from them have the greatest success in involving them in their children's schooling (Caspe, 2003; Hoover-Dempsey & Sandler, 1997). Contrary to what some teachers may believe, parents from all backgrounds have been shown to be open to helping their children learn and do well in school. A review of 51 rigorously designed research studies on parent involvement in schooling concluded the following: "Every study in this review that compared levels of parent involvement found that families of all backgrounds are equally involved at home, although the forms of involvement varied somewhat by culture and ethnicity" (Henderson & Mapp, 2002, p. 61).

Scarpaci (2007) notes that "deciding when to accommodate a student's cultural preference and when to push the child toward assimilation into the larger community is a decision that teachers must make with the utmost care" (p. 47). This is a morally challenging decision. Without understanding the family's child-rearing and educational goals, the teacher can undermine the entire home-school relationship, not to mention the parents' social control over their own child. It should not be necessary for students to forgo home values and to defy parental expectations in order to function successfully in the classroom. Much of current research and theory is, in fact, centered on the belief that people can—and routinely do—function biculturally (see, for example, Padilla, 2002). Knowledgeable teachers can co-construct—with students and families—classroom environments that reflect students' cultural values as well as values of the dominant culture.

COLLECTIVISTIC PARENTS' ORIENTATION TO CHILD REARING

Numerous studies have revealed common denominators in the child-rearing goals of parents from collectivistic societies (see Delgado-Gaitan, 1994; Lewis, 1995; Nsamenang & Lamb, 1994; Reese, Balzano, Gallimore, & Goldenberg, 1995; Tapia Uribe, LeVine, & LeVine, 1994; Valdés, 1996; and Whiting & Whiting, 1975). Despite many differences among the societies represented in such research (Mexican, Japanese, Mexican American, West African, and Kenyan, among others), they share a common goal: moral children who maintain strong bonds to and respect for family. Family is important in all cultures, but in collectivistic families the meaning of family is expanded because the primary developmental goal is a child who will hold family well-being as his or her ultimate priority.

Research conducted with 121 families of immigrant Latino kindergartners showed that parents believe it is their primary responsibility to raise good, moral, respectful children (Reese, Balzano, Gallimore, & Goldenberg, 1995). One mother in the study said, "One has to teach them to be good, aside from schooling. Teach them to be correct [in behavior]. Teach them morals, teach them to be good, because they can have studied a lot, but if one hasn't taught them correct behavior, in the end it [study] doesn't help them" (p. 65).

Similarly, Valdés found in her ethnographic study that even very young children were

> . . . expected to get along with their siblings and not to see themselves as the focus of their mother's existence . . . [A]dults were considered to be more important than children, and children did not expect to control either their mother's attention or her interaction with others. . . . Young children who constantly hung on their mothers were considered to be "*ninos molestos*" (bothersome children), and mothers who gave signs of catering to such behavior were chastised by members of the family as being at fault for not teaching them better. (1996, pp. 120–121)

Fostering teachers' insights into this collectivistic perspective on child rearing and schooling was a primary goal of the professional development associated with the Bridging Cultures Project. Now we turn to a discussion of how teachers actually responded to learning about the collectivistic values of families.

CHANGES IN TEACHERS' RELATIONSHIPS WITH FAMILIES

The most substantive change documented among the Bridging Cultures teachers vis-à-vis families has to do with their relationships with family members. As a result of the project, they have established more mutual and personal relationships with families—relationships founded on greater understanding and respect.

Bridging Cultures teachers repeatedly told us how their perspectives on families and on themselves had changed as a result of the professional development provided through the project. "Learning about a collectivistic orientation helps me to have more of a sense about how a parent from such a background might think and feel, what kind of expectation the parent might have of me as teacher," said 1st grade teacher Pearl Saitzyk. "It fosters more empathy. [I see] how important it is to have background information about the parents that allows us to make parents comfortable in the school environment." According to Mrs. Hernandez, changing the way she views families has helped to solve many potential problems with students. She said, "I am more patient with parents now, and I look deeper into the 'why' of things and make less assumptions."

Mr. Mercado came to recognize that his good relationships with families were based on more than his Spanish proficiency. "I always had good rapport [with families]," he observed, "but now I understand why, and I can maximize, strengthen, and reinforce it now. I understand what I am doing right."

CHANGES IN TEACHERS' APPROACHES
TO PARENT INVOLVEMENT

Bridging Cultures teachers have increased and improved parent-school communication, both formal and informal, through a variety of strategies. They have changed the ways they conduct open house, parent meetings, and parent-teacher conferences. The teachers now understand why parents often ask, "How is my child behaving?" before anything else in parent-teacher conferences. They know that if children are well behaved, parents believe they have done a good job in preparing children for school. So when this question comes up, they take parents' cues and address behavior first, rather than moving directly to academic concerns.

Using Informal Communication to Establish Relationships

Teachers used informal communication to learn more about students' families and to demonstrate a more collectivistic approach to parents. In a sense, they were engaged in ethnography, learning about cultural perspectives directly from members of a culture and taking a nonjudgmental stance. The following examples show how teachers conducted informal communication with parents under strikingly different situations—the first in a school whose policies fostered such interactions, and the second in a school whose policies inhibited them. Ms. Daley reported the following about the urban school where she teaches:

> One of our school rules directs the teachers to accompany their students to the exit gates and to remain there until the parents arrive or until the gate is closed. I take this opportunity to have mini-conferences with the parents. These conversations may never even deal with the child. They may touch on the weather or any other social topic. It may even be just a simple greeting. Yet I find that these interactions foster a closer bond with the parents. (Trumbull, Rothstein-Fisch, Greenfield, & Quiroz, 2001, p. 77)

Across town, the new schedule for Mrs. Hernandez's kindergarten class reduced her opportunities for informal contact with parents. Parents dropped their children off early in the morning, and at the end of her morning session, she had to rush to eat lunch at a time when she would have preferred to have a few minutes with the parents who were picking up their children. Because she believes parent contact is a priority, she adhered to a personal policy of not turning parents away, no matter when they showed up at her classroom. "I have told parents that if they need to talk with me, they can come in, and I'll step away and meet with them," she said. "It may be the only time they can meet me. . . I don't tell them, 'Oh no. You've got to make an appointment.' I always make time to see them." Mrs. Hernandez said she shares experiences about her own children with the parents, follows up on things the parents have shared with her, and asks about siblings who were in her previous classes. "But I try to keep the relationship professional," she noted. "I don't get into the buddy-buddy relationship with them."

Her final comment makes a point that other teachers have made: although they have more personal exchanges with parents than they may have had in the past, they still maintain their professional role as teachers—something that is actually quite harmonious with a collectivistic perspective in which the teacher is an authority and worthy of respect.

Reaching Out via Telephone Calls

Face-to-face contact is not always an option. Early in the project, Mrs. Pérez recognized that because nearly all of the parents of her 3rd grade students were employed in agriculture, they often had difficulty coming in at the beginning or end of the day for informal conversation. Yet she wanted to increase her communication with families to show her support and appreciation, so she began to use telephone calls in new ways. Before the Bridging Cultures Project, she had called parents only when a problem arose, perhaps only two or three times a semester.

Now I call to congratulate them when their student gets "student of the month," [or to tell them] that the child is really improving, when they do something wonderful, as well as when there is a problem . . . It is a very big difference. I really strive to stay more connected. It is all that importance of family. (Trumbull, Diaz-Meza, Hasan, & Rothstein-Fisch, 2001, p. 29)

However, telephone communication obviously requires a common language. Mrs. Pérez's ability to communicate via telephone would be impossible if she were not fluent in Spanish. Without the help of an interpreter, a telephone conversation between a Spanish-speaking mother and an English-speaking teacher would also be impossible.

Moreover, not every Latino family speaks Spanish. This issue came up at a Bridging Cultures meeting. One of the teachers told of another teacher who had tried to conduct an informal conversation with a mother whose child seemed virtually aphasic. When the teacher tried to speak with the mother to learn more about the child, she found communication with the mother equally challenging. The teacher knew that the mother was from Mexico, and yet she did not respond to even the simplest questions in Spanish about the child or her family. The teacher reasoned that the mother must be "retarded," just as the child appeared to be. Later someone suggested that the mother might not speak Spanish at all, but perhaps spoke one of the many indigenous languages in Mexico. When this turned out to be correct, the school made efforts to find someone who could interpret for the teacher and the parent.

Another permutation of the communication problem occurs when the teacher is conversational in Spanish, but the parents want to communicate what they can in English. Both the teacher and the parent share the desire to communicate in the other's language, to show respect and to gain practice in the language of home (from the teacher's perspective) or in the language of school (from the parents' perspective) (A. Werth, personal communication, July 2006).

Teachers may want to try speaking English with parents at first, recognizing that many parents may still be making efforts toward developing their English proficiency. If the communication between the teacher and the parents becomes hampered and the teacher is proficient in Spanish or any other home language, then it is wise to use the language of greatest common proficiency. In so doing, teachers and school personnel acknowledge the family's attempt to learn English.

The family's English learning can also be supported with family literacy programs. These programs will give them extra practice with other families who have the same goal. The teacher can approach this topic by saying something like, "I've seen many families who have had a wonderful experience getting to know other families who are trying to learn English through our family literacy program on Wednesday nights." However, teachers should be careful not to put off parents' attempts to use English in the moment, as if to say, "This is not the time or place for you to practice your English. Go to a class." As with all communication, in any language, it's important to pay attention to nonverbal cues about the other person's understanding and comfort with the conversation.

OPEN HOUSE

Gathering families for open house or Back-to-School Night (typically early in the school year) is a common way to involve parents in their children's education. Given the busy schedule of most families (and particularly those who may work several jobs or have more than two children), rethinking the traditional open house format may be critical for making a favorable first impression (Weinstein & Mignano, 2003). Open house can be a wonderful opportunity to establish two-way communication, or it can be a hurried and overly scripted affair, with administrators and teachers taking a pontifical posture by emphasizing what parents need to do for the school without asking what parents want for their children and from the school. The latter situation is not desirable if teachers are seeking to promote communication and parent involvement.

The typical agenda for open house includes a quick overview of academic goals, standards, and schedules, and suggestions for how parents can augment school learning at home. In some cases, the agenda may include an exhaustive list of other topics, including social and personal expectations for students, the grading system, issues related to homework, discipline procedures, and housekeeping rules (Jones & Jones, 2007). This much information could easily overwhelm parents, especially if they have limited knowledge of U.S. schools.

The topic of parents helping their children with school work at home may be particularly problematic for some parents, who may perceive this as inappropriate. As we have said, this expectation conflicts with the expectation that most immigrant families may have: that the parent's role is to rear well-behaved and respectful children, not to be their children's second teacher (Valdés, 1996). Not only is this something immigrant Latino families may reject as their responsibility, it also may be beyond their current level of ability, given the often limited access to formal education in rural areas where many immigrants lived before coming to the United States. Parents may also have limited proficiency in English, which would make homework help impossible.

Open house may also exacerbate communication barriers—even with well-intentioned bilingual teachers—if the teacher uses technical language that may be unfamiliar to most parents; an example is terminology connected to statewide assessment, such as *standards*, *stanines*, and *portfolios* (Harry et al., 1995; Sosa, 1997). Another example is the concept of a *scoring rubric*, which may not be comprehensible for many parents, serving to confuse them rather than help them understand their child's progress. The same is true for jargon and acronyms such as API (Academic Performance Index) or NCLB (No Child Left Behind).

Although these kinds of hindrances present challenges, they are not insurmountable. The Bridging Cultures teachers came up with a number of innovations to make open house a more welcoming event for immigrant families.

Open House as a Family Photo Opportunity

To promote interest in attending the schoolwide open house, Mrs. Pérez asked her 3rd grade children to tell their parents that she would be taking family portraits that evening. In addition to thinking of a way to entice the whole family to attend, Mrs. Pérez provided materials for the children to craft their own handmade personal invitations. "There is power in their words when they write the invitation," she said. "It is just as important as having something professionally done from the computer." In producing the invitations, she noted, "the students are learning how to write a letter or use an invitation. They use it to bring the families in."

The children's personal invitations to their parents initiated a home-school link. Once family members were in the classroom, Mrs. Pérez demonstrated that she valued their presence by taking photos of them. The photos served two purposes. First, she created a family bulletin board that served as a visual reminder to the students that their families are esteemed. Having photos of family members in the classroom may be especially powerful for recent newcomers to the United States who are experiencing their first few months in this country.

The second function of the photos came later, when Mrs. Pérez realized that family photos could be used as a prompt for writing. Using the digital family images on the computer, the students wrote stories of their migration. When families came back to the classroom for a subsequent parent meeting, they could see their children's work related to their family. Even parents who did not speak English could understand that the children were using their family as a source of knowledge that was appreciated by the school. When parents feel welcome in the classroom, they are more likely to participate in parent activities (Delgado-Gaitan, 1994; Trumbull et al., 2001).

Show What You Know

Mrs. Hernandez also crafted a novel strategy for fostering understanding and relationship building with families right from the start. She realized that it could take weeks or months to learn about each family individually, so at the beginning of the year, during kindergarten orientation, she took the half hour she had with her parent group (after a whole-group orientation in the cafeteria) to develop an "ethnography chart." She distributed seven sticky notes to each family and asked parents to write only their name and their child's name on each sticky note. She knew that some parents were not literate, particularly in English, but she expected that they would be able to write their own and their child's name. She had seven questions posted on large chart paper (see Figure 3.1), which she read aloud one by one, allowing parents to place their names under those questions for which they would answer "yes."

FIGURE 3.1

Questions for Parents at Kindergarten Orientation

Is this your first child in school?
Do you have any other children at our school?
Do you read or write in English?
Do you read or write in Spanish?
Is there anybody to help with English homework at home?
Do you work in or out of your home? [Put up name if you work outside of the home.]
Would you like to volunteer in our class?

Source: From "Parent Involvement in Schooling—According to Whose Values?" (p. 61), by E. Trumbull, C. Rothstein-Fisch, and E. Hernandez, 2003, *School Community Journal*, 13(2). Reprinted with permission.

Mrs. Hernandez reasoned that the parents, who are all Latino (many also immigrants), might feel more comfortable answering some questions in the group rather than being put on the spot individually. Their participation in this group-oriented activity seemed to confirm her assumptions. She was able to use the resulting chart of sticky notes to make decisions about how to work with the families and how to target additional information she needed.

Because one of the obstacles to home-family partnerships is parents' embarrassment about their own lack of formal education (Valdés, 1996), an alternative strategy might be to conduct a dialogue at open house about parents' common experiences—identifying countries of origin and shared concerns about the education of their children. Then targeted conversations among similar subgroups—all those from El Salvador, for example—could be organized, with subgroup members invited to gather in different areas of the room.

These examples demonstrate how a group experience that incorporates the informal and social aspects of communication can be initiated at open house or Back-to-School Night, despite the event's limited time frame. Forging a sincere and caring parent-teacher connection benefits more than good classroom organization; it can serve the larger goal of cultivating multiple sources of support for academic success. As an added benefit, the establishment of meaningful relationships among families at the start of the school year can be an asset for solving chronic problems such as poor attendance, as we discuss in a later section of this chapter.

PARENT-TEACHER CONFERENCES

Parent-teacher conferences are time consuming and challenging for many teachers. They can be redundant and tedious, and are usually scheduled at a time immediately following the preparation of report cards. In addition, they are often fraught with emotion for everyone involved.

Parent-teacher conferences were among the first practices that Bridging Cultures teachers changed. Mrs. Eyler exemplifies an evolution in teachers' perception. Early in the project, she reflected on her dawning awareness that she, and not just her "diverse" students, has a culture. She recalled an incident from a few years earlier:

At one of my first parent conferences at Hoover kindergarten with a mother and her friend or sister—two women—I said to them, "You are the first teacher of the child," and I remember the two women looking at each other, and it landed with a thud! I thought I was being so wise, but they just went, "What?" in a nonfriendly way. They thought I was shirking my responsibility. (Trumbull, Rothstein-Fisch, & Hernandez, 2003, p. 56)

Mrs. Eyler's observation shows her recognition that different cultures may have different ideas about the roles teachers and parents should take. She said that one of her goals in participating in the Bridging Cultures Project "was [to] relate to parents in a better way. I think I was always good, but it is much better now because I don't come to them like they are ignorant. [I'm not] patronizing."

One of the empirical studies that provided the foundation for the project, as described in Chapter 1, explored nine naturally occurring parent-teacher conferences between immigrant Latino families and their children's grade teacher, who is European American (Greenfield, Quiroz, & Raeff, 2000). This research was presented in the course of the initial Bridging Cultures training to provide real-world examples of home-school conflicts that the individualism/collectivism framework could explain. Elsewhere, we have written about how conferences became powerful communication tools for the project teachers (Quiroz, Greenfield, & Altchech, 1999; Trumbull et al., 2001). In this section we offer a few highlights.

Group Parent Conferences

Ms. Altchech began to experiment with parent-teacher conferences after recognizing that the popular format of student-led conferences might be incompatible with Latino culture because it puts children in a position of assuming authority rather than of showing respect for their parents and teachers as authority figures. Here is her account of how she redesigned parent-teacher conferences:

To incorporate the concept of collectivism, I redesigned my parent conferencing into group conferences. For families who couldn't attend, I arranged a separate time. I divided my children by ability levels and language into one English-speaking group and two Spanish-speaking groups . . . I explained the report card format and the meaning of the marks and discussed my expectations for the next quarter. I also discussed what I could do to help students progress academically as well as how the parents could help at home . . . A comfortable and warm feeling came across during the conferencing. Many parents had questions that benefited the others . . . The group conferencing was relaxing for the parents. It was a less threatening environment than the individual style; parents supplied support and were company for one another. This format provided a group voice for the parents rather than an individual voice. After one hour, parents could sign up for a private conference or ask a few questions privately. My new format was successful. I saw all 28 parents in three days. The conference design impressed my principal, who asked me to lead a staff development program on the subject. I see this conferencing format as an evolving process. (Quiroz, Greenfield, & Altchech, 1999, p. 69)

Conferences for Families Whose Children Are Bused to School

Scheduling conferences can be difficult, even in the best of circumstances, but when children are bused across a large urban area to a distant school, the challenges are even greater—especially for families with many children. Several years after the project started, Mr. Mercado's class included 16 students—about half the class—who were bused in, yet he was determined to meet with every family. Here's how he described his thinking and actions to deal with the situation:

I realized I had to go to them. So I took a day off from work (not easy to arrange, but possible) and went to their neighborhood. I was able to get a classroom at a year-round school that had some teachers off-track at the time. I scheduled all 16 parents between 7:30 a.m. and 4:30 p.m. I introduced myself, and they told me about themselves. We always start with chit-chat. I've been to all but three of the Latin American countries, so I can talk with them about places and foods. I ate lunch with some parents, looking for commonalities with the purpose of creating bonds. It takes the teacher off the pedestal . . .

Goals begin with what the parent feels the child needs . . . We talk about a wide spectrum of things. We write the goals together and list strategies for achieving them. I use a piece of carbon paper so that we each end up with a final document. I set it up so that there's a list of all the areas to improve and a list of all the areas of strengths . . . Four months later, I bring the original sheet to the next conference, and I start crossing out the goals that have been accomplished, so the parents can feel the progress. Some parents have told me, and this is with a child in 4th–5th grade, that their child has gone all five years without the parents ever meeting his or her teachers. The child may have never been referred for assessment, yet children come to me unable to read or not having been tested for gifted. I'm shocked this year that two students have been recommended for special education in the 5th grade. (Trumbull, Rothstein-Fisch, Greenfield, & Quiroz, 2001, p. 70)

Mr. Mercado's mobile conference was cited by his principal as an example of positive practice during the school audit in 2002. Because the principal recognized the value of this commitment to improve relations with parents, the school decided it would provide transportation for all the parents to attend a special open house. Now parents with children in all grade levels take a bus (with children ages 5 and older) from their neighborhood school to Mr. Mercado's school.

Parent-teacher conferences need not be a series of hurried 15- or 20-minute exercises in frustration. Bridging Cultures teachers have constructed numerous ways of making conferences a more positive experience for all. In particular, they honor collectivistic values by making social relationships between parents and teachers a priority and the first step in creating shared supports for students' success. The examples of teachers' innovations illustrate the linkages among cultural understanding, organizational changes, and new relationships with families that can lead to better home-school coordination over time.

HOME VISITS

As another way to understand students and their culture, Bridging Cultures teachers began making home visits. First-grade teacher Pearl Saitzyk described some of her experiences:

> I think it was more harmonious after it boiled down to the understanding of what is going on. That changed me. I felt more connected. One thing that was different that year [the first year of the project] was that I was invited to birthday parties . . . I went . . . It just added more depth [to my relationship with parents]. I went to one child's home, and there was no furniture. I came there, and there was a child sleeping on the floor in the corner. I had an extra bed, so I brought it over . . . (Trumbull, Rothstein-Fisch, & Hernandez, 2003, p. 55)

Although home visits may seem like—and often are—a good way to reach out to families, it is important that teachers take cues from parents about the kind of personal contact the parents want. Mrs. Pérez would like to visit each child's home, but she listens to parents' messages:

> I've let the children know that I'd be happy to come if they invite me . . . I've made some home visits. I just sit and talk

with the parents. I tell them if they can't come to the conference, I would come and do a home visit. Some parents have thanked me for offering . . . and they prefer a phone conversation. The parents' situation would be sad, and they don't want me to see it. And I know that because I would have died to have a teacher come to my home. (Trumbull, Rothstein-Fisch, & Hernandez, 2003, p. 55)

HOMEWORK

Although the merits of homework are contested, the benefits can reach beyond the simple acquisition of knowledge (Cooper, 2001). Homework can help develop study habits and foster responsibility. In an idealized form, homework engages parents in the supervision of their children's work by involving them in the processes of establishing work ethics, managing time, and consolidating new concepts. But in reality, parents often feel inadequate to the task (Hoover-Dempsey, Bassler, & Burrow, 1995), and the expectation of parent engagement can be even more problematic for parents who have limited if any fluency in English and may be unfamiliar with U.S. schooling practices and philosophies (Delgado-Gaitan, 1992).

When teachers or schools instruct parents to establish a fixed homework time, to have their children sit in a quiet, well-lit area, and to ensure that homework is checked each evening, they are not being realistic. Among immigrants, it is not uncommon for several families to share an apartment intended for one family, eliminating any possibility of a quiet space for solitary study time. Moreover, if there were such an area, the student might not want to be isolated from the family. Separation would be considered punitive rather than purposeful in accomplishing homework goals.

Despite the obstacles (and some of the debate about homework in general), Bridging Cultures teachers have developed a number of strategies to help support students' successful completion of homework. Using the group as a resource, homework challenges have been reduced or eliminated.

Homework Packets

In the year-round school where she taught, Mrs. Eyler's kindergarten class was getting ready to go "off track" for about four weeks. She gave the children homework packets, introducing the concept by saying that one of her two coteachers had made the packets especially for the children. They cheered in response. As she discussed each assignment and previewed the skills they would need to complete it, the children clapped their hands and told the teacher "thank you." From a collectivistic perspective, the homework was situated in the context of their teacher's care for them. The homework seemed to be more like a gift from a caring adult rather than an intrusion on their vacation time.

Group Homework Practice

During an observation in Amada Pérez's 3rd grade classroom, a reading group had just completed their oral language lesson when Mrs. Pérez distributed the homework sheet. It required fitting spelling words into the story they had just read. With Mrs. Pérez as a nonparticipating member of the group, the children read each sentence and decided via consensus which spelling word (in English) fit in each sentence. The children were only allowed to use their fingers to follow along; they did not have pens or pencils. The observer asked, "Was this because the parents might not be proficient in English to help at home? Was this a result of the Bridging Cultures Project?" Mrs. Pérez said, "Yes," and added that the students' English proficiency was improving as a result of the project. The English homework was "nonthreatening" now, "because of the group experience," she said. "It's fine because they can do it. They know their spelling words and can complete it at home without help. When we go over it orally, they can all have success."

Group homework practice had multiple benefits for the students. First, they had an immediate opportunity to apply what they had just learned in their reading lesson, expanding their understanding of the reading material to a new context. Helping each other and sharing answers in a small group of similarly skilled students provided a low-risk opportunity to contribute answers. When students appeared unsure of their answer, the group quickly discussed the matter and decided, via consensus, on the right answer—and they could provide an explanation for why it was correct. It is highly unlikely that the same higher-order reasoning skills would have occurred if the students prepared their answers independently at home. Enhanced memory skills were fostered within a social context—one that might have particular meaning for the students from collectivistic backgrounds. Finally, more students turned in completed homework assignments because doing homework was not a traumatic experience. Instead of triggering what students couldn't remember, doing homework was a time when they were able to recall the earlier instructions and responses, probably because they had shared a socially engaged experience.

Two years later, Mrs. Pérez added another layer to her approach to homework. The students' desks were organized in clusters of four. Each cluster maintained its own daily homework file. As part of the morning ritual, the teacher asked if everyone in the four-person group had put their homework in the group folder. As each group responded that they had done so, everyone clapped. It was true in every case during our observation. Mrs. Pérez reasoned that the students would never want to disappoint their team, so the homework return rate soared to 100 percent. She used the power of the group to ensure that homework was completed consistently.

Homework Delivery

According to Marie Altchech, whereas she formerly had to ask for a volunteer to write down homework assignments for absent students, in her more collectivistic classroom, now it "happens automatically. Now children remember who is sick; they take the initiative to write [the] homework [assignment down] and even deliver it to the child." It's possible that by the 4th grade these students may have been socialized at school to protect their own tasks and not consider the needs of others (Raeff, Greenfield, & Quiroz, 2000). But perhaps with Ms. Altchech's approach to create a more balanced individualistic and collectivistic classroom, their natural inclination to think of others returned. Ms. Altchech recounted her surprise when a previously absent 4th-grade student returned to school with all her homework completed. When she asked the student how this happened, she replied, "My partner brought it to my house."

When classrooms are organized to foster group responsibility, teachers' work becomes easier. Managing the various issues associated with homework becomes inconsequential when classrooms build on the concept of group support. The same is true for attendance.

ATTENDANCE

Attendance is not typically considered a classroom management problem. A number of popular books on classroom management do not include the topic of attendance in the subject index (Jones & Jones, 2007; Levin & Nolan, 2007). This omission is hardly surprising, insofar as absences may actually make classroom management easier because of a lower child-teacher ratio.

However, consistent attendance is important to the functioning of a cohesive classroom group. When children attend school regularly, everyone shares the rules and norms of the class, and activities and scheduling have continuity. In contrast, when students are absent, they miss out on opportunities to absorb classroom expectations as well as the content and process of learning, making it more likely that the teacher will need to resocialize them to classroom expectations and respond to questions about "what's going on."

Bridging Cultures teachers have used their knowledge of collectivism to find ways to improve attendance. Attendance-related experiences have emerged as topics during project meetings, interviews, and observations. The first example that follows describes how a teacher's understanding of families actually changed her views of why children were absent and resulted in vastly improved attendance. The second example raises questions about the need for extrinsic motivation for perfect attendance. The third shows how the group typically responds when a student is absent.

Solving the Attendance Problem

Mrs. Eyler observed that many students in her school were absent—some quite frequently. Some of her colleagues held almost cynical views about the likelihood of enlisting parents' help in addressing the problem. But Mrs. Eyler recalled discussions in Bridging Cultures meetings about the strong value of helping and cooperation associated with collectivistic cultures, and she decided to approach the parents of her immigrant Latino students. She simply asked several mothers what they thought could be done to help children get to school more consistently, conveying the sense that this was a *group* concern by saying, "We have a problem." The mothers worked together to build a network of parents who could walk each other's children to school if an emergency (such as the illness of an infant) prevented the parent from doing so. In the school neighborhood, it was not safe for young children to walk to school alone. The mothers solved the problem, and Mrs. Eyler's relationship with them was strengthened. As a result, she resolved to work more closely with parents on other problems (see Trumbull, Rothstein-Fisch, Greenfield, & Quiroz, 2001).

Communicating the Importance of Attendance

In the past, Mrs. Pérez tried to improve attendance by awarding stars to the whole group for perfect attendance. With her knowledge of Bridging Cultures, she realized why this method didn't seem to work. She reported, "[The children] didn't really care that much about the stars; they only cared about having perfect attendance. They didn't even ask for the star . . . it didn't matter . . . it was just the idea that everyone was there." Mrs. Pérez also said that the children felt sad for their absent classmates and were eager to volunteer to get the homework to a sick friend. She said, "Before Bridging Cultures, I don't remember that happening too often." Instead, she recalls parents coming in to get the homework, as opposed to the situation now where children want to help.

This is an important example that illustrates how the teacher's extrinsic rewards for improved attendance fell flat as a motivator. Her students were not interested in earning stars, but they were highly motivated to help their fellow classmates return to the group. Prior to the project, Mrs. Pérez might have assumed that the children were just not interested in attendance issues, as evidenced by their lack-luster desire to earn stars, but she would have been wrong. With her understanding of collectivism, she could forgo the need for little gimmicks and leverage the students' own needs to have their group together.

Making an effort to reach out to absent children was also evident in Mrs. Hernandez's class. Returning from recess one day, the children gathered in the computer lab. Mrs. Hernandez asked, "Who is missing from our class?" The children replied, "Joel," and the computer-based lesson centered on the production of get-well cards for him. Mrs. Hernandez instructed the children, who were in kindergarten and 1st and 2nd grade, to "pick four pictures that Joel will like to have on a card. If you don't know how to do it, raise your hand." We observed the children helping each other first and then raising their hands if they couldn't figure out what to do.

These examples illustrate how a focus on the group helps support attendance—a responsibility that elementary school teachers typically assume belongs exclusively to parents. The last example also illustrates how a lesson on the computer can be used in service to the group, maintaining a social orientation while learning technological skills.

PARENT VOLUNTEERS

Parent volunteers can help with classroom management in myriad ways. But teachers need strategies for organizing parent participation in the classroom, and choosing good strategies depends on cultural knowledge. Parents can support students' work at learning centers, read to children, listen to them read aloud, and help with routine clerical duties. In busy, crowded classrooms, extra help can bring welcome relief, but the role of parent volunteers in Bridging Cultures classrooms has special meaning.

Mrs. Hernandez has been developing, modifying, and documenting innovative ways to increase parent involvement since the beginning of the Bridging Cultures Project, when she indicated in her exit survey that such involvement would be one of her goals. We provide a brief overview of her innovations here. (For a more in-depth description, see Trumbull, Rothstein-Fisch, Greenfield, & Quiroz, 2001; and Trumbull, Rothstein-Fisch, & Hernandez, 2003.)

Fostering Increased Parent Involvement

Mrs. Hernandez initially sought parent volunteers to help her with an escalating amount of work. "I thought the whole burden of teaching was mine. I would stay long hours after school doing what I needed to [do to] get my kids ahead. But my needs, combined with new understandings [from Bridging Cultures meetings], led to new steps" (Trumbull, Rothstein-Fisch, Greenfield, & Quiroz, 2001, p. 85).

First, Mrs. Hernandez decided she would transcend her fears of having parents observe her. Then, understanding that formal education is often limited in parents' home countries, Mrs. Hernandez began to engage parents in simple conversations to determine how much schooling they had and how they might be able to help in the classroom and at home. Next, she welcomed younger siblings into the classroom along with their parents, acting on the assumption that the young siblings of her kindergarten, 1st, and 2nd grade students would benefit from the experience. (In observations, her expectations seem to have been born out, when, for example, older students read to the younger ones and included them in songs and games.) At conference time, she showed parents a folder she had created with a variety of classroom volunteer tasks, including those that seemed to match each parent's ability. Describing the folder, she said,

I included a paragraph about how much I needed them to help their children achieve different academic goals . . . I typed a page addressed to each individual parent in which I explained whom they could work with and what skills to focus on. I also included a page with other activities that weren't necessarily academic that they could all help me with. (Trumbull, Rothstein-Fisch, et al., 2001, p. 86)

As a result of her efforts, the number of volunteers in Mrs. Hernandez's classroom increased from 1 to 12 from the 17 families represented in her class. The volunteers' responsibilities ranged from supporting students' reading (and, in the process, modeling appropriate reading skills for other new volunteers) to sewing costumes for a schoolwide program. One parent became the school-community liaison.

Several years later, and at another school, Mrs. Hernandez faced new challenges in recruiting parent volunteers. More mothers were working outside of the home, limiting the number of mothers who were available to volunteer, and a mandated, highly scripted Open Court reading curriculum made it more difficult to use parents to help with reading activities. Mrs. Hernandez responded by meeting with working parents at times convenient to them and engaging them in creating materials that could be used in the classroom and at home. However, the circumstances of the new school and the new curriculum continued to keep the number of classroom volunteers low, despite her previous successes at a different school. Clearly, even some of the best practices won't work if the setting doesn't match the practice. Ultimately, schoolwide policies can either support or inhibit parent involvement that supports classroom functioning (Trumbull, Rothstein-Fisch, & Hernandez, 2003).

Parents as Guest Speakers and Resources

Mrs. Pérez acknowledges that many parents are unable to volunteer regularly in her class. However, maintaining open, informal relationships makes parents feel comfortable coming into her class in other capacities, allowing her to use them as valuable resources. She described how one father came into the classroom to talk about his work. "He owns a used car lot. He brought prizes and asked questions. It was amazing. I just asked him to tell his story—how he came, and how he progressed. He had never done it before and he loved it!" Her example reminds us of the practice of uncovering families' "funds of knowledge" as resources for students' learning in the classroom (Moll & Gonzalez, 2004).

Developing a trusting relationship with families—through formal and informal means—is the first step toward gaining their support for classroom orchestration (see Chapter 5 for more information). Once that trust is achieved, families can be enlisted for many kinds of help, just as Bridging Cultures teachers have demonstrated—from helping neighborhood children get to school to volunteering in the classroom. But sometimes, before seeking to develop trust, it is necessary to give parents explicit information about how schools in the United States operate. In the next section, we show how Bridging Cultures teachers have approached parents with this information and how they balance collectivism and individualism in their classrooms.

INDIVIDUALISM AND COLLECTIVISM: TWO VALID CULTURAL ORIENTATIONS

In addition to recognizing that they need to understand parents' cultures better, the Bridging Cultures teachers know that parents can benefit from an understanding of the culture of schooling in the United States. As a result of their increased awareness of the potential conflicts between home and school cultures, teachers began to talk with parents more explicitly about school practices and policies and the rationales for them in cultural terms. As mentioned, some teachers have designed parent workshops and used the individualism/collectivism framework to highlight why the school has certain expectations, and they invite parents to talk about their own perspectives. Others have introduced the topic in conversations or conferences, or in the context of a particular incident. All the teachers in the project agree that parents deserve to have and can benefit from a greater understanding of school culture. They also believe that parents need to meet the school halfway and that students need to acquire a dual-cultural perspective and the ability to function in the cultures of both school and home (Trumbull, Rothstein-Fisch, & Hernandez, 2003).

Explicit Explanations

Elvia Hernandez, herself an immigrant Latina, has experienced the clash of cultural value systems in her classroom, so she has tried to make the differences (and the interplay) of individualism and collectivism explicit. "I told the parents at an inservice [session] about individualism and collectivism, and my goals and values about individualism," she said, "[because] one of the things we teach is individualism in little ways, and we need to prepare them for this. Parents have become aware of the importance of responsibility and independence in the classroom."

Parents and teachers may have different assumptions about how children should behave, but new norms of behavior can be taught without denigrating parents' values. Mrs. Hernandez used her personal experience to help parents accept the need for a certain amount of cultural change:

> I've come to think that I want to help the parents . . . learn more about what is expected of them and their children in society here in the United States. I want them to know that I accept them and I came from the same roots they did. We're immigrants. For a while we didn't have legal status here. We share that. I want their children to be bilingual. Let's get them a good base in English. I want the parents to know what the reality is. They have to learn English. . . . Basically a little bit of how society works and what's expected of them. (Trumbull, Rothstein-Fisch, & Hernandez, 2003, pp. 63–64)

As an immigrant herself, Mrs. Hernandez has taken the position that parents need to acculturate to dominant norms, yet she accepts their cultural values in the ways she works with them and their children.

Using Parent Meetings to Explain Individualism and Collectivism

Catherine Daley used her parent meetings to help make parents more aware of the culture of the school, and, in particular, how the school values related to individualism differ from those of collectivism. Together the teacher and parents have forged their own cultural bridge. In Ms. Daley's view, "We have a right to not negate [students'] culture but also not to negate the American culture that their parents want them exposed to as well. So neither should be negated. Both should be accepted and explored" (Trumbull, Rothstein-Fisch, & Hernandez, 2003, p. 64). She communicates this perspective—of the need for students to have bicultural skills—to parents as they discuss the topic of culture.

SCHOOL POLICIES AND CULTURAL CONFLICT

In this chapter, we have described some instances in which school policy encouraged parent involvement, such as in Ms. Daley's school, where the requirement that teachers walk their students to the gate provides the opportunity to chat informally with parents. In other cases, school policies may create huge obstacles to parent involvement. Mr. Mercado provided an example of the latter situation.

For security reasons, the district where Mr. Mercado's school is located implemented a lockdown policy; that is, schools would be locked, and anyone who wanted to gain entrance to them would need an appointment and personal identification. The district also banned baby strollers from all schools—from the buildings as well as the schoolyard. "Mothers with infants would [now] have to find someone to care for their baby or park the stroller and get a chain to secure it—which is another hindrance for parent participation,"

Mr. Mercado said. To make matters worse, teachers and parents were battling over parking spaces, which were limited in number. Teachers arriving after a certain time would find the lot full; they attributed the problem to parents parking in what should be *their* spaces. A couple of the teachers began putting flyers on offending parents' cars saying, "Do not park in our parking lot."

These factors added up to an unwelcoming stance toward parents. As Mr. Mercado said, "We don't want to discourage them from coming to school . . . We complain that parents don't come to school . . . but we have been sending these [negative] messages out." Parents were, in fact, extremely upset and came in as a group to meet with the principal. Mr. Mercado continued, "I urged the principal to explain to the parents why this [policy] was happening and explain to staff why the [parents] were acting this way." According to Mr. Mercado, "It was a very hostile meeting, with parents saying, 'How dare you lock us out from where our children are all day?'" No one had told the parents why the district had mandated the lockdown policy or the stroller policy. Once the principal explained the reasons, with the help of a translator, understanding replaced mistrust and anger. Because the principal knew of Mr. Mercado's involvement with Bridging Cultures, she prevailed upon him to explain the situation to the faculty in a short after-school presentation.

Mr. Mercado has frequently found himself in the position of cultural broker, trying to sensitively explain to colleagues why a conflict might be occurring. A kindergarten teacher in his school complained that too many parents were coming in and out of her room. They were interfering with her ability to teach, she said, and they "needed to cut the [apron] strings." When Mr. Mercado explained his interpretation of the situation, suggesting that the Latino parents' behavior came from the cultural value of the family staying together, the teacher became less angry and "maybe more sympathetic. She couldn't allow them in, but she greeted them with less anger and made them feel less unwanted," according to Mr. Mercado. On another occasion, Mr. Mercado ventured an explanation for parents' preference to voice their concerns as a group rather than individually to the principal as a "combination of respect for authority and their natural group orientation" (Trumbull, Rothstein-Fisch, & Hernandez, 2003, p. 63).

School Breakfast as a Context for Conflict

As a result of a discussion about cross-cultural miscommunication related to school breakfast programs that came up during a Bridging Cultures meeting, Ms. Daley interceded with a similar schoolwide policy problem at her school. Ms. Daley's school, like many others, has a federally funded school breakfast program. Family members (parents and younger siblings) are not allowed to sit with students during breakfast or lunch because regulations stipulate that all food is designated for enrolled students only. For families who value closeness and sharing, this policy must seem absurd.

Frustrated with the constant stream of parents coming into the cafeteria during breakfast and the consequent threat of losing funding, the school posted a sign (in English and Spanish): "Only students permitted in eating area." Parents, mostly mothers, were insulted and angry and marched as a group to the principal's office to complain. The school's perspective was that the food "belonged" to particular students and (perhaps less overtly) that parents were babying their children by helping to feed the younger ones. From the mothers' point of view, families share everything, and helping young children models a value of helping and caring. Assumptions, based on cultural perspectives, were rampant but unquestioned, no doubt on both sides.

When Ms. Daley heard that this problem was developing in her school and that administrators were ready to take action, she intervened by going to the bilingual coordinator. The coordinator wrote a letter to parents explaining the district policy and assuring them that it was meant to protect their school-age children's access to free breakfast. She also expressed the school's desire to involve them in other school activities and asked for their support. Rather than the stark sign posted, as previously described, friendly signs decorated with children's drawings were displayed. Because the communication was based on better cultural understanding, no parents objected to the policy.

Ms. Saitzyk observed that learning about parents' values of helping, sharing, and keeping the family together led her to a better understanding of why it was so hard for parents of young children to "sit on the sidelines [at breakfast time] while their children were struggling with their little milk containers. I was able to explain it to them in a way that they didn't feel offended. Then they were pretty good about sitting there."

All of the project teachers have intervened on students' behalf to see to it that the school system works better for them. For example, Ms. Altchech visits the middle school her students will be attending to talk with counselors and teachers there about the strengths and needs of students. Her concern is that their capabilities may be underestimated in the new educational environment, where they are likely to get less personal attention and cultural and linguistic sources of difference may be overlooked, dismissed, or simply regarded as intellectual deficits. She also talks with parents about how to advocate for their children so that they get what they need at the next level of schooling.

◆ ◆ ◆ ◆ ◆

Equipped with the Bridging Cultures framework, teachers have demonstrated agility in constructing new ways to bring home and school together in ways that are culturally relevant for families, that improve classroom organization and orchestration, and that are educationally meaningful. Demystifying U.S. schooling is an important step, but when teachers think that the cultural shift must be unidirectional—moving from family belief systems to school belief systems—they miss the opportunity to take advantage of all the strengths that collectivistic families offer, such as keeping the family together, helping and sharing, and working as a group with common purpose. This situation seems particularly ironic given that these family-based strengths are among those often cited as contributing to students' resiliency and school success (see Benard, 2004). Classroom management shifts to classroom orchestration when teachers understand the likely origin of students' behavior, as we will see in the next chapter on helping and sharing.

HELPING AND SHARING—
DOING WHAT COMES
NATURALLY

Mrs. Pérez: "You have two things to do. One is in Spanish and one is in English."

Children: [Moan]

Mrs. Pérez: "But what if I tell you [that] you can help each other?"

Children: [Cheer]

As we have noted, the well-being of the group is the most fundamental collectivistic value. In this chapter, we take a closer look at two prominent ways people contribute to the welfare of the group: helping and sharing. We describe teacher practices that capitalize on students' inclination to help and share. Of course, these themes come up in other chapters too, because helping others, whether in the context of the group or assisting individuals, was prominent in all Bridging Cultures classrooms.

HEADING OFF POTENTIAL CONFLICT

Helping and sharing—seemingly so important for well-organized classrooms—can cause problems if the tacit values of the teacher and students differ. When teachers and other school personnel are not consciously aware of these differences, they may construe students' helping each other not only as off-task and unproductive but, worse, as cheating (discussed further in Chapter 7). Even sharing a book or a pencil can be seen as enabling an irresponsible student to continue forgetting required materials.

In general, helping others learn in the context of U.S. schools is the teacher's exclusive domain. When confusion or questions arise, students are often instructed to "raise your hand and continue working" until the teacher can respond. Yet students may be unable to "continue working" on assignments that are confusing, and any number of disruptive behaviors, from fidgeting to talking to getting out of seats, may follow. Disorder and chaos can result when students are unclear about their task and the teacher is busy helping others. Figuring out how to proceed may become even more difficult if the student is not proficient in the language of instruction. The answer to the question "Who can help?" seems unnecessarily narrow if the only answer is "the teacher." When only the teacher can help, confusion can escalate to the point that children swarm around the teacher asking for help. (Incidentally, swarming occurred only once during 40 hours of observations in Bridging Cultures classrooms.)

As we discussed in Chapter 1, a study that included asking students, their mothers, and their teachers about responsibilities related to the classroom job of cleaning the chalkboard evoked different responses from the three groups. In that study, Latino immigrant parents believed that children should defer their own task in order to help a sick classmate. This response conflicted with the teachers' predominant response, which involved finding a third person and maintaining the integrity of task completion (Raeff, Greenfield, & Quiroz, 2000).

The example from the study shows how decisions about helping others can present inherent cultural conflict between individualistic schools and collectivistic families. The situation of children waiting for help from the teacher suggests the potential for a similar conflict. From an individualistic perspective, there is the need to comply with the teacher's directions to wait for her help—being careful not to talk and to generally stay out of trouble. However, collectivistic students may have deeply ingrained tendencies to get help from others or to offer it to those who appear to need it. The irony of this conflict

is that learning how to help others is a standard goal of the popular "character trait" programs proliferating across the United States
(Fallona & Richardson, 2006; Lee, 2005).

Unless teachers make explicit their rules for helping, and unless
they begin to understand and then to use the full capacity of helping as a service for learning, teaching, and classroom organization,
students with collectivistic values will continue to be confused or
punished for misconduct. However, for teachers to accept the kind
of helping that some students naturally engage in, they may have to
alter their ideas of how learning takes place and how knowledge is
constructed. An individualistic orientation to knowledge and learning
implicitly holds that both of these are the purview of the individual.
The notion that knowledge is group-held (which is the prevailing
belief in many cultures) or that learning is not necessarily an individual process is likely quite alien to most U.S. teachers.

TEACHERS' CHANGED PERSPECTIVES ON HELPING

The Bridging Cultures teachers changed their perspectives on helping
and sharing as a result of understanding the cultural values of individualism and collectivism. For Mr. Mercado, "it was just being aware of
the differences. You know, so many times where we're doing things
in the classroom already, and suddenly it's been given a name. And
you're like, 'Oh, well, I was doing that, but now it has a name.'"

The following example (first described in Trumbull, Greenfield,
Rothstein-Fisch, and Maynard, 1999) illustrates how Mr. Mercado
used a history lesson to support the meaning of "helping" in students' collectivistic cultures.

THE VILLAGE

A presenter from the Museum of Science and Industry came to visit a
4th–5th grade classroom to share items representing the colonial period
in American history. The beginning of her talk emphasized how important

the concept of "village" was to the colonists, specifically, "how everybody worked in the village and everyone contributed to the village." With that in mind, Mr. Mercado began using the concept of "village" to identify times when helpfulness was either observed or needed, such as with classroom chores like cleaning the chalkboard trays or organizing the classroom library into fiction and nonfiction. Mr. Mercado reported that the visitor's use of the word and description of the colonial "village" was an important marker because "...if I hadn't had that initial awareness [of Bridging Cultures], I really wouldn't have tied it into the present-day classroom situation."

In Mrs. Eyler's kindergarten classroom, she noticed that her students had a strong desire to help each other, but she didn't understand the depth of their commitment. Once she understood how the children's cultural values affected their orientation toward helping, she found that her job became easier because students could support classmates, perhaps even better than she could. "The children are always wanting to help their friends," she said. "Academically or in cleaning up, it was always there. I was conscious of not telling them 'don't,' but I didn't respect it or understand it. I [was] kind of stepping over them—not in a mean way, but not in an understanding way." Once she understood the cultural value of helping, she encouraged it. "Instead of me getting up to help a student, I get the students to do it—to speak to them. 'Maybe you can explain it better.' Then they help, step-by-step; instead of my doing it or another teacher, they can help someone else."

Helping as a Priority

Soon after returning from winter break, Mrs. Hernandez gathered her class of kindergartners and 1st and 2nd graders and began discussing the concept of New Year's resolutions that people make to improve themselves. She started the conversation by describing what she wanted to achieve for the following year. She had three goals, including visiting her brother and spending more time with friends.

She asked the children to share their resolutions for themselves on how to be a better student. Here are the top seven responses:

1. Help others.
2. Listen to the teacher.
3. Learn numbers.
4. Pay more attention to the calendar.
5. Do homework.
6. Listen to the teacher when she explains assignments.
7. Pay attention to the class during computer time.

The first item on the list, "Help others," was students' overwhelming priority. They apparently believed the best and most important thing to do was assist others. This was seemingly more important and fundamental to their own academic progress than their subsequent suggestions, such as improved attention and listening, which are more readily associated with improved learning. The students perceived that their first responsibility was to attend to the needs of others, even before they focused on their own learning. The sincerity of their intent was demonstrated by the fact that no discipline problems occurred in the class during six hours of observation.

Did the resolution to help others emanate more from the students' collectivistic backgrounds (very likely), the teacher's understanding and support of collectivistic values (with the potential to use that understanding and support to increase helpfulness), or the mixed-age group (and the possibility of 1st and 2nd grade children helping the kindergartners in their class)? It's impossible to know the causes for the children's emphasis on helping, but it is striking that in an already cooperative and harmonious classroom, the children wanted to help even more. As an aside, we should mention that the multiage classroom is probably a more natural learning environment for children who have siblings and cousins helping younger family members at home.

During an interview with Mrs. Hernandez, she described some of the other instances of helping among her students. "They help tie each other's shoes, help figure out answers to problems, and help put away backpacks; they help new students adjust, especially if they don't speak any English."

These children took the initiative to help each other, showing that students can organize themselves to solve problems without direction from the teacher. Rather than undermining this process in favor of promoting behaviors, such as "let her do it herself," the teacher sanctioned the value of helping others.

CLASSROOM MONITORS

Monitors are students who help with a wide variety of classroom chores, such as passing out papers, distributing balls for recess, helping the group line up for lunch, and cleaning the chalkboard. The usual arrangement is one person per job, and frequently the names of monitors and their duties are displayed in classrooms to minimize disputes over whose job it is to do any number of tasks. Bridging Cultures teachers began to rethink the assumption of "one student, one job." Speaking of the evolution of practice in his own classroom, Mr. Mercado said, "I had individual monitors, and now [I have] group monitors, and that works more smoothly than what I had before. I am just more conscious about why certain things work. I have very good management; everyone has responsibilities." He noted that even after being absent and leaving the class with a substitute teacher, he can walk in the next day and "everything will look wonderful."

Mr. Mercado's successful use of group monitors comes about because he discusses the need for classroom helpers at the beginning of the school year, asking children, "Why do I need help in the classroom?" The children answer that his job is "to teach." When he asks them what kinds of assistance they can provide, they offer to manage the books, clean the rooms, erase the chalkboard, and do other chores. He engages the students in discussing why two people are more efficient than one, particularly if one is absent. He makes his thinking transparent to his students because he believes that they will help in appropriate ways if they help construct those ideas and understand why they are important.

Mrs. Pérez also made a change in her use of monitors. "I used to be very resistant to having more than one child out of the classroom at once. It would bother me when they asked for a friend to go with them to do an errand," she said. After her involvement in Bridging Cultures, she began to let students leave the classroom with a friend, and, she reported, "it has never been a problem." Students almost always ask if they can take a friend, Mrs. Pérez noted, and she now accepts their preference. "Yeah, of course, it is much better to have someone with you. I had never thought of that [before], and I was just resistant to it. They just go and do their thing and come back. It has been consistent; they never go alone except to the bathroom."

Similarly, Mrs. Pérez changed her policy about class leaders, with co-officers filling each position, instead of one student per office. Thus the class has two presidents—one boy and one girl. The officers function somewhat like monitors. One walks in the front of the line and one in the back when the class goes somewhere as a group. They also accompany students to the office, if needed.

A slightly different picture emerged in Ms. Daley's 2nd grade class. About two years after the initial Bridging Cultures workshops, she reported in a meeting with other project teachers and the core researchers that she had given up the whole idea of monitors. In the beginning she told her students, "If someone is done, help someone else. We're not done until everyone is done." She reported that her students asked for certain jobs, and her response was to open the process of distributing classroom chores to the whole class. At the time, that system seemed to work well.

However, two years later with different students, her approach to monitors had to be modified. During an in-depth interview, she reported that her students' acculturation toward increasing individualism—either from their experience in school or from their lives in a densely populated urban area—seemed to have led them to expect individual monitors. Her students now seemed to identify with the "one student, one job" rule. In the following example, Ms. Daley describes what happened.

IN SEARCH OF A PERFECT SYSTEM

I had a problem with monitors. It was hard for me to remember who they were. If someone was unable to do their job, they became very insistent to be the only ones to do the job. [They were] very territorial . . . I have resolved it—no more monitors. Everyone can help as long as they want to. Some kids always want to be the one to pass out papers. Some kids have been in the country longer, and they are the leaders and want to be in charge. Everyone wants to pass out papers and pencils, but nobody likes to do the menial jobs—erase the board or put down the chairs. But when I ask them, then they all want to do it.

Well, everybody can help. I give them the freedom to say, "I did my part." I'm aware of the children who think, "Let someone else do the work." Those are the kids that are asked, "Can you please take the chairs down?" Then other kids will offer to help. I pray that kids like that will see it isn't an awful chore and [think], "Thank goodness, someone else helped me."

This example demonstrates the influence of mainstream individualism, perhaps as a result of previous teachers' telling students that they *cannot* help each other, or that once a single task is completed, the student is not responsible for any other classroom chore but his own. Both of these approaches can work against classroom harmony and cooperation. However, when the whole group is seen as potential helpers, then it may be that the "power of the group" is still at work, because when "the other kids will offer to help," those who are reluctant can be motivated by their peers. In a two-year span of time, the problem with monitors seemed to recur in Ms. Daley's classroom, indicating that something as simple as identifying the whole class as helpers might still be confusing for some students.

However, in her class of kindergartners and 1st and 2nd graders, Mrs. Hernandez reported that the "children all clean up and everybody helps. [It's] not just job specific." This approach seemed to solve any problems with classroom monitors in Mrs. Hernandez's class.

The discussion of whole-class monitors—with everyone responsible for everything—is a good place to stop and reflect on the fact that what may work well in one classroom may fail miserably in another. As we have said all along, the Bridging Cultures teachers have generated their own practices, and these keep changing on the basis of many variables, not the least of which is having a new group of students every year and having new immigrants arrive at various times in the academic year. In general, teachers have shifted from a "one person, one job" approach to having the whole class work together to complete classroom jobs or to assigning multiple monitors.

We offer a final note on Ms. Daley's own development as a teacher. During one observation, she asked a student to get the beanbags for a physical education assessment, and the student requested that a friend go with him. Before her involvement in the Bridging Cultures Project, she may have construed the student's request as inappropriate because it would deprive two children of the lesson that was underway instead of just one, or she may have thought that a second helper could become a catalyst for fooling around in the hallways or in an unsupervised classroom. Instead, she understood that the student simply preferred to get help even when it wasn't necessarily required, and she quickly gave permission to allow him to select a friend to go along. The two children returned promptly with the beanbags for the class.

LEARNING PARTNERS

Establishing learning partners is a good way to promote helping (McLeod, Fisher, & Hoover, 2003), while simultaneously freeing up the teacher to assist others. Establishing the partnerships is usually accomplished by carefully organizing seating arrangements for optimal matches (Jones & Jones, 2007). In Ms. Altchech's 4th grade class, seat partners are available for help when she is busy teaching. "There are other people to help—the people nearby—and [they can] suggest how to find words in the dictionary or share homework," she explained. This action was observed frequently in her classroom. In one instance, she had just read a story about kiwi birds and instructed her students to "fold their paper like a book and write, in full sentences, the evidence from the story that indicated that the kiwi was a 'funny bird.'" The students were to work in teams to complete the task.

Circulating around the room, the observer noticed variations in how the students worked in pairs. In some cases, one child did the talking and one did the writing. In other pairs, the students appeared to work independently but occasionally checked to see what their partner had written. Other pairs discussed whether or not a particular concept (such as the fact that the kiwi is the size of a hen) fit the category of "funny."

During recess immediately following the kiwi story task, Ms. Altchech was asked about the impact of the Bridging Cultures Project on teaching and learning in her class. "I always believed in children's need to work together and share their answers because it validates their thinking." However, she was quick to report that the framework of individualism and collectivism had provided "theoretical support for group work, especially with the Hispanic students. It makes sense because they do that in class anyway."

Learning partners are also very common in Ms. Daley's 2nd grade class. In one instance, the children were working on preparing a globe of the world. She showed one child how to do it and then told him, "Now you will do it to help your partners." When a student asked her, "Who is my partner?" she responded by saying, "All the children in the room." Describing the incident, Ms. Daley said, "I do that constantly with my students. I will teach one child, and from then on, it is up to them to work well together. I tell them, 'You cannot work alone in the real world. You have to help others.'" Although Ms. Daley's definition of "partners" is not as formalized as two students assigned by the teacher or self-chosen to work together, the underlying idea is the same. Partners in the class are essential as learning and teaching resources. Each child has the potential to be the partner of every other child.

Learning partners are also prevalent in Mrs. Pérez's classroom. On one occasion, she was previewing some math worksheets for her 3rd grade students. She referred to the problems as "story problems" (rather than "word problems"), consciously or unconsciously using a term reflecting students' inclinations to tell family stories. She also shared her own personal experience in solving story problems and described being nervous when she was confronted with such problems. She had difficulty with them, she said, but she offered her students a way to address the challenge: "Wouldn't it feel better if someone could help you?" she asked. The children responded in unison: "Yes." She then said, "Put your name on the paper and the name of the person helping you on the paper. Put a circle around your name, but put your helper's name on it too." In this way, she honored the partnership by documenting the relationship. In addition, with this kind of record keeping, she could troubleshoot problems if both students were unable to solve the problems successfully as a team.

The use of partners is so routine in Mr. Mercado's class that it is virtually automatic. During one observation, a child was seen working on an assignment intended for pairs. Because her partner was absent, she worked collaboratively with the other two students in her table cluster. However, when she was writing up her contribution, she put both her name and her partner's name on the book, although the partner was absent throughout the entire assignment. When the observer asked why she did that, she replied, "Because she is the one that is always my partner." Thus the importance of acknowledging one's partner as a helper was evident even when the partner was absent. The perspective revealed in this example parallels the perspective of family members toward each other: though a member is absent, he or she is still present in everyone's concept of the family.

Buddies in the Classroom

Several teachers have begun using class buddies—a variant of learning partners. What is the difference between a buddy and a partner? In some cases the terms are interchangeable. Whereas partners are often determined by seating assignment, in the case of buddies, stronger students may be identified to help those most in need of extra support. At other times, buddies are older children from upper grades who come to help. However, in practice this distinction may be moot, as some teachers may always refer to helpers as "partners" or as "buddies," regardless of the task or relationship between students. In addition, the terms can refer to both the helping partner and the partner being helped.

In Chapter 7 we explore in detail the use of math buddies in the context of an assessment example from Mrs. Pérez's classroom. We describe it briefly here because it so effectively demonstrates the importance of helping.

Mrs. Pérez was disappointed in her students' proficiency with timed multiplication facts; many had not mastered facts at the level expected in 3rd grade. She asked the class what could be done about this problem. The students volunteered to help their peers who were having difficulty. Their goal was to have everyone know the facts, so they established "math buddies" to practice the timed facts and to support each other (albeit silently) during individualized testing.

Earlier in the project, Mrs. Pérez used the same concept of allowing students to help each other. At that time, she was referring to helpers as "tutors" rather than "buddies." As she gathered students on the floor, she said, "Some of you are going to have to share books. Who is going to be Brenda's tutor? Who is going to be Saul's tutor?" This pairing was for three distinct buddy pairs, and the students were eager to share their materials with their classmates.

Older Buddies

Several Bridging Cultures classes developed buddy relationships with other classes in their schools. Mrs. Eyler's kindergartners enjoyed the help of two 5th graders who worked in her classroom every day when they were off-track. The 5th grade students benefited from the structure of being back in school, and their desire to help others was met. In addition, Mrs. Eyler reported that the families supported the concept of their children serving as helpers with a safe, regular place to go when they were off-track. The older students, several of whom stopped by during an observation, seemed to occupy a special place in the classroom. Once they arrived, they immediately helped clean up the art and writing-supply areas. As a reward for all their work during the semester, Mrs. Eyler and her coteacher took the older students out for an evening of fun that included dinner and a movie. Mrs. Eyler commented, "It was expensive, but I felt good about taking them out for an extravagant evening to thank them for helping in the classroom."

Mrs. Hernandez also benefited from the help of older students. During one visit, observers watched the buddies from a 4th–5th combination class arrive, eager to help with reading. Each child in Mrs. Hernandez's class had a reading buddy who made monthly visits to the public library to collect books for their little buddies. Mrs. Hernandez explained that, according to their teacher, the 4th and 5th graders still stumbled in their oral reading, so the relationship benefited them as well: the older students could read without fear of embarrassment and model their determination to achieve mastery in oral reading proficiency. In addition, older siblings or cousins could be the buddies of the younger students. At least two family pairs read a lot together—one was a set of siblings, and the others were cousins. They read together for 15 minutes twice a week. The older buddies were trained to keep their younger buddies' story interest high and to relate the topics from the book to their own experiences. In many cases, younger children read chorally with their buddies.

This cross-class buddy system offers many advantages. First, older buddies have a vested interest in going to the library for the purpose of helping someone (and this interest may be even greater when their little buddy is a relative). Second, the practice benefits both students in the pair by providing increased time to practice reading together. Third, the practice frees up more time for the teacher to help those who may need special attention or to coordinate common buddy activities with the other teacher. Mrs. Hernandez reported a fourth benefit: the buddies may continue to work together beyond the allotted classroom time—such as at home, in the case of relatives.

HELPING IN MODERATION

Like all classroom activities, helping has to be closely monitored. Sometimes partners can become crutches for students who fear making an effort on their own. As we have said, students need skills to work well within groups *and* independently. Ms. Daley pointed out how too much helping can become a problem as she described a boy in her class who was constantly looking for help from other students, particularly a student named Bryan. "I have told Bryan that he can share with the other boy, because he is learning, and we [do] work together [much of the time]," she said. When Bryan says that his classmate is copying, the other boy says, "No, we are sharing," Ms. Daley reported. But she added that there are times when she says, "Now I want to know what is in your brain by yourself."

SHARING AMONG STUDENTS

Teachers often emphasize rules about where and how students can keep personal items. It is not uncommon for teachers, particularly in the lower elementary grades, to place a small box or bin in the middle of each table for materials to be used by everyone in the group. This strategy "eliminates the need for students to borrow these supplies from one another, and it reduces the need for a trip to out-of-group storage areas" (Evertson, Emmer, & Worsham, 2006, p. 115). This arrangement seems motivated by the need to eliminate problems that occur as a result of conflict over personal property. However, many students may actually prefer to share materials in the first place, when that practice is culturally harmonious with expectations in the home environment. In our discussion of sharing within the Bridging Cultures teachers' classrooms, we include the sharing of objects as well as the sharing of knowledge and experiences.

As with some other collectivistic practices we discuss, many teachers no doubt had a norm of sharing in their classrooms before their encounter with the Bridging Cultures Project. For them, the project has given them greater faith in their intuitive knowledge and led to an expansion of existing collectivistic practices related to sharing. Other teachers have consciously revised ways of responding to students' culture-based proclivities. Mrs. Eyler discussed how her views and strategies changed. "There is *one* propeller in the Legos. I used to say, 'He had it first,' and then tell them to take turns. Now I say, 'You need to find a way to share it.'" Mrs. Eyler's emphasis on sharing is particularly notable because, as a kindergarten teacher, she represents the children's first contact with elementary school culture, and home-school conflict is likely to be most pronounced at this time (Pianta, Cox, Tylor, & Early, 1999).

According to Ms. Daley, sharing is non-negotiable. "I refuse to have anyone say this is *my* desk or *my* crayon . . . It belongs to all of us, because it is part of the school. We are all responsible." The children in her class demonstrate their desire to share in ways similar to those of their home environment, as evidenced, for example, in how they view food. Here is how Ms. Daley described snack time:

> When my kids bring snacks, it is a banquet. They don't bring three cookies; they bring the entire package. They bring econo-size chips. When the kids need to share, they take what is in the home [that] they have [in] the largest size possible . . . They bring the large sizes intentionally to share with others . . . It is expected. "You brought the snack; I'll help you eat it." I have never had a child complain about sharing. I have had children say, "I had so many friends around me, I had only two chips." I have to say, "Be sure the person sharing gets their share too."

Sharing is evident even among 4th graders who have received all their education in the United States. During an observation in Ms. Altchech's class, a student had borrowed a pencil from his friend. The lending friend sat unoccupied as others began their writing task. When the observer asked why he wasn't working, he said he didn't have a pencil because he had lent it out to someone in need. Then the student who had the borrowed pencil asked yet another student for a pencil for the first student, and the problem was solved.

Although sharing the pencil delayed the student's ability to work on the academic task at hand, the gesture illustrates how readily students share and get help in doing so from others. In total, the entire sharing incident occurred over less than two minutes. According to Ms. Altchech, "As the children get older, the kids want their property. They have their individual supply boxes, but they are very quick to share when someone else needs something. I never see a problem with 'This is my box, my pen. You can't use it.' The boxes are just a physical place to keep things." She noted that she never had to ask the students to share. "It is automatic. It is part of their mode of thinking."

Likewise, Mr. Mercado reported that students in his 4th–5th grade combination class still share materials, even though they are becoming more accustomed to having their own possessions. "My kids bring their own pencil cases with stickers. They don't want to use the group cardboard ones. They will definitely share their own boxes, but not like, 'It is mine, not yours.'"

SHARING WITH THE TEACHER

Ms. Daley's students are eager to share with adults as well as classmates. According to Ms. Daley, they want to bring her things, and although initially she resisted these gifts, she has found that it is important to accept them graciously. When the school started to sell snack foods, the students would typically buy something, such as juice or a cookie, and offer it to her. She would suggest that the students share it with their friends, or, realizing how important sharing is for the children, she would make a point to eat their offerings in front of them after making certain they had enough to eat themselves. During a visit to her classroom, the observer noted how eager the children were to share. Just before class, she received a gift from one of the students, a stuffed animal, which she told the children would remain in the classroom. Then, just moments later, she received a Disney-character bank. She gave the gift giver a big hug and said, "This will be our official class piggy bank."

In both instances, Ms. Daley was aware of the importance of sharing for the children, and yet she herself did not want to be singled out. Her strategy was to accept the gifts graciously and then to be sure that they were shared among the whole class. In this way she honored the children's need to share while reinserting the objects into the group for the whole class to enjoy.

Incidentally, the children also wanted to share something with the observer. When two girls returned from recess, they brought the visitor a pink plastic pencil box. The observer, the first author, keeps that pencil box as a symbol of their generosity and kindness. It is a constant reminder of how ingrained sharing and inclusiveness is for children from collectivistic homes.

Sometimes children share materials that may be intended for a single person or a special use, but Ms. Daley reported that she does not have any problems with theft in her class. She commented that her students know what belongs to the school, "so if someone tries to take [something belonging to the school] home, others will help and intervene." This is an excellent example of how the group regulates the use of what is intended for sharing (school materials) and what may be a personal item. Weinstein and Mignano (2003) cite cultural variation as a possible source of confusion about the meanings of "sharing and generosity" compared to "private ownership" (p. 341). As in other situations, we recommend a teacher-led discussion to clarify matters—in this case, a discussion in which the students talk about the differences between sharing and stealing, providing personal examples and cases from their own experience. Making assumptions about even "temporary property," such as materials that belong to the school but are used for a period of time by one child, can lead to problems and disruptions in the classroom.

SHARING AS PART OF A REWARD SYSTEM

Students' desire to share objects can supersede the significance of the object to the individual. Mrs. Hernandez described how some other classrooms at her school set up a reward system:

[Students could earn] fake money with the teacher's face on the money, with $500 or $1,000 for older children and $1, $5, [and] $10 for younger [children]. The children save their money, and then they bid for things at the end of the week. One group said, "Let's put our money together," but they would only get one toy. They always gave the money to their banker. When they purchased something, they thought about what they could buy to share. In the case of a coloring book, they wondered about ripping out the pages and thus turning the book into worksheets and not a book at all.

What would happen if the teacher required the children to keep their own money and did not allow them to share? This would suggest a very individualistic orientation. Teachers with this orientation would not subscribe to the described practice of sharing, particularly if one of their goals was to encourage individual motivation or competition. They might reason that students need to keep their own reward money for themselves—thus learning a lesson in capitalism and private enterprise; or perhaps the notion of destroying a book in order to share it might cause a teacher to intervene and halt the idea of pooling funds. Conversely, thinking of ways to motivate students who have the desire and skills to share (and help) would create a more congruent learning environment for students with collectivistic backgrounds. Rewards and motivation are explained in more detail in Chapter 5, but for now, we will simply state that we have found that extrinsic objects may be less effective motivators for collectivistic students, and, moreover, the use of objects as rewards could undermine their inclination to share as well as learn.

SHARING NONMATERIAL THINGS

Sharing goes beyond objects. It also encompasses sharing of time, skills, knowledge, and experiences. According to Mrs. Pérez, she allots more time to share information, skills, and objects from outside of school as part of her English language learners' curriculum as a result of the Bridging Cultures Project. She reported that she is "making more time for sharing and not feeling guilty about it." Instead of incorporating sharing "as an afterthought or a once-in-a-while thing, now [it is] a regular part of the real curriculum. Seeing the connections . . . and being more aware of the theoretical framework support my decision for choosing certain activities."

During one observation in Mrs. Pérez's 3rd grade classroom, the whole group sat on the rug for an hour as students shared objects from home. They had been organized into groups before the observation, and it was the "share day" designated for one particular group. The following example describes the activity in this class with many English language learners.

SHARING EXPERIENCES

Mrs. Pérez organizes her "share days" by dividing the class into groups of about four students each. On the designated share day, students from certain groups are encouraged to bring something to discuss with the whole class. It is intended to be a rich language arts experience that engages students in asking and answering questions about their special objects. During one observation, a student was sharing an art box, and the teacher prompted the children with the English words for "wite-out" and "oil pastel." At the end of the lesson, the teacher said, "I have two things to share; tell me what you want me to share. I have pictures with Ms. Singer in the desert. How many want me to share the desert first? I also have pictures of my favorite people in the whole world." The students recognized that the album she was referring to contained pictures of them. "It's us!" they exclaimed. Nevertheless, they decided they wanted to see the pictures of their teacher rather than photos of themselves. The desire to hear about the teacher's trip and to learn from her experience relates to what we described in Chapter 2 regarding the inclusion of adults as part of the classroom community.

Like Mrs. Pérez, Mr. Mercado has found that sharing experiences in class requires some organization. Storytelling can become enormously time-consuming if not planned for properly. Whereas Mrs. Pérez organized her class into groups that shared on a specific day, Mr. Mercado found that sharing in small groups was a viable alternative to whole-group sharing. In one case, the students were very eager to share their stories about their grandmothers (described in Chapter 2). "When I did the grandmother stories, it got way out of hand," he commented. "I used something I learned from our Bridging Cultures meetings. I had them talk with the people at their table for five minutes. I rotated 'round the classroom and listened to each group."

Carter and Doyle (2006) point out that sharing time typically means "giving the floor to a single student at a time with the task of spontaneously composing and telling a personal narrative about his or her out-of-school life" (p. 387). They cite three difficulties associated with this practice. First, the discussion can meander, and the demands on a teacher's ingenuity in guiding the conversation and his or her knowledge of the content increase accordingly. Moreover, bidding for turns and turn allocation can demand considerable teacher concentration as well as student skill in gaining the floor, though there are sociocultural differences here. Second, there is fear that only a few students will be concerned with what the speaker is saying, allowing the rest of the class to lose focus. Third, the content of the sharing may not be germane to the topic. As a result of these things, teachers often take control of the content (Carter & Doyle, 2006).

What we have seen in the Bridging Cultures classrooms is a variety of harmonious ways to allow students to voice their ideas, sometimes with the whole group, sometimes in smaller groups, and sometimes in pairs. No single way is best, and, overall, using a variety of strategies may be the best course to follow. In every case, some kind of structure and organization is helpful, as the Bridging Cultures teachers have found out.

◆ ◆ ◆ ◆ ◆

Unless teachers understand how much students from collectivistic families value helping and sharing, they may waste a lot of time and energy attempting to prevent students from helping each other, rather than turning the inclination to everyone's advantage. Based on our observations in Bridging Cultures classrooms, we believe it is possible to marshal the values of helping and sharing to the benefit of the entire classroom. When students must work independently, the teacher can explain how to do so and why it is desirable. The necessary classroom management strategy is to be explicit and to discuss the contexts for each type of task—when it is appropriate to help and share and when it is appropriate to work independently.

In Chapter 5 we present more examples of helping and sharing, but the applications are directly linked to the concept of classroom orchestration, including rule setting and discipline.

CULTURALLY RESPONSIVE CLASSROOM ORCHESTRATION

Traditionally, strategies for classroom management have been derived from an individualistic psychological orientation. As such, classroom management is about correcting and preventing disruptions caused by the "difficult" students and about reinforcing positive comportment of the well-adjusted ones. Such defensive reactions reflect a conception of classroom relationships as single and frequently unidirectional interactions between the teacher and individual students.

—Rachel A. Lotan, "Managing Groupwork in the Heterogeneous Classroom,"
in *Handbook of Classroom Management*

In this chapter, we explore how Bridging Cultures teachers have used their understanding of students' culture-based values and strengths to choose strategies that result in smooth orchestration of their classrooms. We use the term *orchestration* rather than *management* throughout this chapter because it denotes bringing about harmony—with all the members of the classroom "orchestra" in synchrony.

In contrast to the individualistic and control-oriented approach identified by Lotan in the epigraph that opens this chapter, we describe an approach to students as a group that takes advantage of its sense of community and desire for group harmony. The teachers' strategies for classroom orchestration range from traditional ones, such as transitional activities to help students move from one activity to another, to relying on students' group skills to carry on an activity during a teacher's temporary absence. We discuss the concept of "community" in the classroom because it is implicit in how Bridging Cultures classrooms work. We also address the complex issue of motivation because it is at the root of all classroom orchestration (or management) strategies. Motivation affects students' engagement in learning and classroom behavior, and both are predicated on not only personality differences but also on cultural values.

STRATEGIES FOR HARMONY

Bridging Cultures teachers use a variety of strategies to ensure the smooth running of their classrooms and to minimize interference with learning activities. Our observations revealed overwhelmingly harmonious and productive classrooms: We saw only nine cases of overt discipline in 40 hours of observation! We believe that the extremely low incidence of disruptions or misbehavior resulted from the strategies the teachers constructed with consideration for students' cultural values. These approaches to orchestration proved to be effective because they produced a minimum of conflict between home and school values.

Bridging Cultures teachers use relatively few *observable* management strategies, such as reminding students of class rules. Here is where management and organization merge: in well-selected, culturally-harmonious organization of classroom activity that precludes the need for explicit management or discipline. Harmony in the classroom is accomplished much more through choices in the types of activities and in how those activities are organized. Nevertheless, during observations we did keep a tally of four strategies: redirection, transition activities, nonresponse, and direct discipline. Although these general strategies are likely to be observed in many classrooms, the ways teachers choose to carry them out may look different once culture is considered. For example, an activity that is intended to help students make a transition from one academic focus to another is more likely to involve all students as a group rather than as individuals (see transition activities below). Figure 5.1 shows the number of instances of each type of strategy recorded during about 40 hours of classroom observation.

FIGURE 5.1

Instances of Classroom Management Strategies
Used by Bridging Cultures Teachers

Teacher Strategy	Number of Instances
Redirection—shifting a student's focus from one thing to another	5
Transition Activities—a break to switch to a new activity	6
Nonresponse—teacher's apparent ignoring of a student's behavior	2
Discipline—reprimand or threat	9

Redirection

We use the term *redirection* to indicate the shifting of a student's attention from one thing, such as an off-task activity, to something else, often accomplished by changing the topic of interaction or engaging a student in a new activity to avoid a looming problem. Examples include asking a student, "What do we *not* do?" (as a reminder of what counts as unacceptable behavior, according to Mrs. Eyler) or, "Juan, tell him how you want to be treated" (to help a child gain reentry into the group, according to Ms. Daley).

Transition Activities

Transition activities serve two purposes. They may be used (1) as a break within a period of instruction that requires a lot of concentration, such as listening to a lengthy explanation, or (2) to get children to move from one activity to another. For example, to give students a break from an extended activity, Mrs. Pérez uses stretching games.

To move children from one activity to another, Mrs. Hernandez has them gather on the rug and sing the song "Open, Shut Them," which uses hand gestures. The children clap, put their hands on their laps, and then creep them into their mouths. She has them silently mouth the words to the same hand movements when they come in from recess and need to settle into an academic activity. Likewise, Mrs. Eyler uses songs to get students' attention and to segue to another activity. On one occasion, she led the children in the singing and finger play of "Eensy-Weensy Spider" in Spanish. One child asked to lead the song and was granted her wish. The children clapped for their classmate when she was finished.

Nonresponse

We use the term *nonresponse* to refer to a teacher's ignoring of a behavior in an apparent effort to avoid reinforcing it. At one point, Ms. Daley ignored a child who was chanting another student's name during a physical education activity, although she had previously suggested to the group that such chanting might be distracting to the student who was trying to perform a task.

Direct Discipline

In our more than 40 hours of observation we documented very few instances of Bridging Cultures teachers directly disciplining students. Five teachers *never* engaged in any overt discipline during our visits. In fact, we observed only nine instances of direct discipline, and eight of these occurred in one classroom on the last day of school before an extended break.

Bridging Cultures teachers do regulate students' behavior as they deem necessary. And it is certainly possible that teachers may soften efforts to control students when observers are present. During a debriefing interview, one teacher reflected, perhaps ruefully, that elements of her disciplinary style may have been captured by some of her young students as they engaged in free play one afternoon. According to the teacher, the children were mimicking her, saying,

"Don't move," "Be quiet," "Sit down," "I only want to call your name one time, Diego." This disclosure by the teacher demonstrates that even in the best cases, teachers use a variety of old and new strategies, and they face difficult challenges when the needs of one child eclipse the learning of others, which may have been the case with Diego. Yet in the Bridging Cultures classrooms, we observed children also being encouraged to help each other focus on the work of school and take responsibility for many aspects of classroom functioning, as described in earlier chapters.

PUNISHMENT

Bridging Cultures teachers use a minimum of punishment, though it is not completely absent from their classrooms. One form of punishment used when students are not working well with peers is to offer them the opportunity to work or perform alone. This strategy can help to avoid a problem. For example, during an activity, Ms. Daley asked students to cover their faces but to project an emotion underneath. Instead of following directions, the students first looked around to see what others were doing. One boy immediately broke into a punching and fighting persona. Most of the others did hide their faces but did not project an emotion, or they uncovered their faces perhaps to look around. Four girls conferred with each other about which emotion to express. The teacher seemed unhappy with the responses of some of the students and asked, "Would you rather do it out here [by yourself]?" (She was standing apart from the group). The threat of standing apart from the whole group was an apparent punishment for children who did not want to be separate from their group, and their behavior improved.

When Punishment May Be Undeserved

Sometimes cultural differences can lead to undeserved punishment. Ms. Daley described the following incident during a Bridging

Cultures meeting, and it illustrates how both school staff and students need to learn about and be sensitive to cultural differences.

GUILTY EYES

Two children were accused of a minor school crime and were called into the principal's office. While the principal was interrogating them, one child looked down at the floor, and the other looked directly at the principal. The principal presumed that the child looking down must be guilty, and the child was expelled for a few days.

Ms. Daley knew the expelled boy and did not believe he was likely to have committed the crime. But she also knew that he would be looking down as a sign of respect—not guilt. With that in mind, Ms. Daley decided to make "looking into eyes" an explicit lesson with her class. She had a discussion with her 3rd graders about eye contact. She told the children that different people and different situations required different kinds of looking. She said, "If you are with a Latino, look down, and when you are with a typical American, you must look at them in the eyes." Ms. Daley wanted to be very clear that culture affects how different people interpret the same behavior.

Following the discussion, she took the children on a "field trip" around the school to identify which adults they should lower their eyes for and which they should look at eye to eye. In addition, she cautioned students not to overgeneralize or make too many assumptions by telling them, "If the other person is not getting the right message, try switching the eye contact." (Rothstein-Fisch, 2003, pp. 54–55)

When Punishment May Be a Reward

At times, teachers have kept students in from recess to complete homework (ostensibly as a punishment), but sometimes that practice has not functioned as intended. One child in Ms. Altchech's classroom explained to the observer that she hated recess and actually preferred to stay in the classroom. She may have also enjoyed being close to her teacher. Another Bridging Cultures teacher withheld recess as a punishment for failure to turn in homework, but over time she decided the approach was not constructive. She replaced it with a system in which volunteer students helped their classmates successfully complete missing homework. Thus, the teacher's solution for the infraction shifted from a punitive reaction to a problem-solving strategy.

OTHER ORCHESTRATION STRATEGIES

Pre-emptive Action

At times, it was quite clear that teachers were anticipating potential discipline problems and giving students explicit guidelines about how they could control themselves and thereby prevent an incident. Of course, some students present greater potential for interpersonal problems than others do. For example, one teacher had a student who was prone to disrupting others. She tried to help him think before he acted. "Kenny, are you going to mess him up or are you going to help him?" she asked when she saw Kenny approaching another child who was struggling to check for spelling errors in a paragraph she had just completed. In this way, she was showcasing the option of helping rather than hindering a fellow student's progress.

Tapping Students' Sense of Shared Responsibility

Whereas the emphasis of many discipline programs is on individual responsibility (see Canter & Canter, 1992; Edwards, 2004), the emphasis in Bridging Cultures classrooms is often on group responsibility. Each student is still responsible for his or her own actions, but, in addition, students are expected to help each other remain focused on a task and behave appropriately. For example, during a visit to Mrs. Hernandez's class, we observed a group discussion of the story *The River*. A few children began to chatter during an exchange between Mrs. Hernandez and one student, who was discussing his fishing experiences, but children nearby said "Shh," and the chattering stopped.

Ms. Saitzyk described a situation in which she had to leave her bilingual English-Spanish 1st grade classroom for a few minutes to confer with another teacher. As she stood outside in the hallway, she heard her students continuing the lesson she had begun. Not a moment was lost, and no one misbehaved. Simultaneously, the monolingual English students of the other 1st grade teacher erupted into noisy commotion. Ms. Saitzyk wondered at the time whether the difference was due to students' differences in culture-based socialization practices. Her students appeared to automatically take responsibility for the continuing activity of the group, whereas the students in her colleague's class did no such thing. One explanation for her students' response would be that the children had a culturally rooted notion that working together is rewarding and motivating in itself. This notion allowed them to stay focused on the learning task without external motivators such as rewards for doing the work or punishments for not doing it.

CLASSROOM RULES

All Bridging Cultures classrooms have a short set of rules that are posted in a prominent spot. In most cases, students have been involved in framing the rules, although teachers may shape their final form. Describing her process, Ms. Daley said, "My rules are generic enough that I am able to ask the students what they'd like our rules to be, and after[ward] we discuss and group them into their appropriate categories (such as 'affecting others,' 'being a prepared student'). Then I use the titles of the categories as our rules." Here is a recent set of rules, or guidelines, for her classroom:

- I am the best student I can be.
- I follow directions the first time I hear them.
- I respect others as I wish to be respected.

In the following account, Mrs. Pérez described the process she uses to generate classroom rules, along with the main kinds of rules that tend to result.

MRS. PÉREZ'S RULES PROCESS

I've used this method very successfully with 3rd and 5th graders for many years. On the first or second day of school, we brainstorm rules all together, and I write them on butcher paper where I have drawn a Venn diagram. [The] left side is for "Students"; the right side is for "Teachers" [including classroom aides]; and the middle section where the circles intersect is for "Everybody" [students and teachers]. I put the headings up as we go along, beginning with "Students." Everything the students come up with [is included] . . . Then I explain that teachers also need rules, if we are to have a democratic classroom, and that they can also contribute rules they believe the teachers should follow. They are so surprised to be asked to do this! They usually begin with, "No yelling, screaming, or running." They also believe that teachers should not drink coffee in the classroom. When they are finished listing these rules, we read them all aloud together and vote on which ones are the most important in both lists and underline or circle them. Next, we decide which are the common rules that come up for both students and teachers. We select three to six rules to put in the center section of the Venn diagram. Usually, the main rule is simply "Respect each other." Others that come up often every year are "Do all your homework and turn it in on time" and "Help each other."

Next, the students select the best writers in the class to make a large poster or class chart with their rules under the heading "OUR RULES." Finally, *everybody* signs at the bottom (including teacher and assistant), and it goes up on the wall in a very prominent place.

Every morning (after the flag and world pledges), our rules are recited until they are learned by heart, respected, and followed. There are consequences for breaking the rules set up by the school, [but] our class rules are different than the school rules.

Mr. Mercado also involves all of his 4th grade students in the formation of rules. The following is his account of the process.

MR. MERCADO'S RULES PROCESS

In regard to the classroom rules, I begin the lesson with a make-believe scenario of a place with no rules. I ask the kids what they think would happen. They come up with all the right answers (i.e., total chaos). I then bring it to a smaller scale and ask them to think about a schoolyard with no rules. Again they come up with the answers that I was hoping for. Then I bring it to the classroom level. After we discuss what a classroom with no rules looks like (and, yes, someone always says "murder" in addition to "noise," "hitting," etc.), they generate three or four rules that they think our classroom should have. Generally each group comes up with similar rules, so when I chart them, all are happy and feel validated. The rules this year [2002–2003] are

- Try to do your best work.
- Treat others with respect.
- Do not get out of your seat unnecessarily or talk unnecessarily, especially when the teacher is talking.

This last rule allows students to go to the water fountain, work collaboratively, and the like. If you allow them to generate too many rules, they tend to come up with silly ones or redundant ones. The "respect" word covers a lot.

Mrs. Hernandez believes it is more realistic and practical to frame a small set of rules for her kindergarten and 1st grade students herself. "My students don't really know what a rule is," she said. She explains the idea of rules by reading them the story *Marty the Monkey* during the first week of school. In the story, Marty goes to school and does a series of things he's not supposed to do. "He has to learn basically the same rules we use," she explained, such as not disturbing other students when they are trying to get their schoolwork done and keeping his hands to himself. After she reads the story, she reviews some of the rules with her students. She role-plays with them, and then she puts the rules on a chart. Here is a recent set of rules for her classroom:

- No running in class.
- Raise your hand and wait for your turn to speak.
- Work quietly.
- Share and take turns.
- Be polite, be nice.

Mrs. Hernandez's approach is probably more reflective of the culture of the school than are the approaches of some of the other teachers. Raising one's hand to speak individually is typical of expectations in U.S. classrooms. In the classroom discussion about rules just described, Mrs. Hernandez regulated children's participation—one child at a time. Yet observations showed that she does express a group orientation in other interactions with children and encourages them to help each other (see Chapter 2). She holds out a model of keeping one's hands to oneself, but she allows a great deal of physical proximity among children in actuality. It was in her classroom that children were observed to be stroking a friend's hair, touching feet, or sitting shoulder to shoulder.

Ms. Altchech's rules for her 4th grade classroom (posted in English and Spanish) were documented during a visit about 18 months after the project began:

- I will follow directions the first time they are given.
- I will raise my hand for permission to speak or leave my seat.
- I will keep my hands, feet, and objects to myself.
- I will pay attention.
- I will show respect to all.

Five years later, her rules had become much broader and less behavioral. She displayed only two, which are broad expectations rather than explicit rules (see the distinction made by Johns & Espinoza, 1996):

- Be respectful.
- Be serious about learning.

Some educators believe that rules shaped by the teacher should not be passed off as student-created rules. They argue that the process is a sham (Johns & Espinoza, 1996). "The term [rules] suggest a compliance orientation to classroom management" (Jones & Jones, 2007, p. 197). In this way, they reinforce the power of the teacher and its coinciding opposite, the disempowerment of students. Some teachers have advocated alternative terms such as "rights" (Weinstein & Mignano, 2003, p. 72). Regardless of the term, most teachers would agree that norms, standards, or rules are important for keeping classrooms safe and for promoting optimal learning environments.

The processes that Bridging Cultures teachers described appear to engage students in an authentic way in thinking about the kinds of classrooms they want to have. One can see some variety in the rules and how they are arrived at, but the common denominator is the notion of "respect," which appears over and over in Bridging Cultures classrooms. Respect is a high priority in collectivistic families, and the Bridging Cultures teachers explicitly recognize this priority.

THE MEANING OF RESPECT IN
BRIDGING CULTURES CLASSROOMS

"Respect" (*respeto*, in Spanish) is highly valued in many cultures. In Latino cultures it assumes a broad definition and is perhaps more important than in other cultures that encourage asserting one's own needs and thoughts. In her book, *Con Respeto*, Mexican American researcher Dr. Guadalupe Valdés (1996) explains:

> [The notion of] *respeto* . . . goes much beyond the meaning of the English term *respect*. The English notion of respect suggests some of the elements of the concept of *respeto*,

but excludes many others. *Respeto* in its broadest sense is a set of attitudes toward individuals and/or the roles that they occupy. It is believed that certain roles demand or require particular types of behavior . . . Having *respeto* for one's family involves functioning according to specific views about the nature of the roles filled by the various members of the family. . . . It also involves demonstrating personal regard for the individual who happens to occupy that role. (p. 130)

Mr. Mercado's classroom rule about not interrupting the teacher is reminiscent of the expectations held by the Mexican American parents with whom Dr. Valdés conducted her ethnographic research:

Respeto for the mother's role was very much in evidence in what the children did *not* do. . . . [E]ven children under two years old did not interrupt conversations between their mother and other adults . . . Out of *respeto*, children were expected to wait until their mother was finished with whatever activity she was involved in before they asked for her attention. (p. 120)

The word *respect* comes up often in Bridging Cultures classrooms. We have seen it in classroom rules, as well as in reminders to students and in discussions whose purpose is to resolve conflicts. For example, Ms. Daley reminded her students of the need to be respectful to one of their classmates who was reading aloud from a lengthy composition. "Ryan is writing the longest novel. We will give him the respect he gives to us." Ryan read the book he had written with his face buried behind the large pages. When he finished, the class applauded.

MOTIVATION

Motivation, in the classroom context, can be defined as whatever it takes to get students interested and engaged in learning. Motivation is said to be strongly affected by the degree to which basic human needs are met, such as the need for food, safety, a sense of belonging, or self-esteem (Maslow, 1970). Arguments about the importance of intrinsic versus extrinsic motivation have raged in the educational psychology literature. Some, such as well-known educator Alfie Kohn (1993), insist that the only important motivators for students to learn and achieve come from within. He cites studies showing that both adults and children are more likely to persevere with a difficult task if they are *not* rewarded by anything more than their own satisfaction at completing it (see, for example, Deci, Koestner, & Ryan, 1999).

Academic motivation comes from a variety of sources. It may arise from social needs. With social motivation, students are said to seek peer acceptance and approval and to avoid social rejection. According to a review of the literature, "The positive academic effects of emotional support from peers are well documented. Students who perceive that their peers support and care about them also tend to be more engaged in positive aspects of classroom life than are students who do not perceive such support" (Wentzel, 2006, p. 633). However, this perspective does not necessarily take into account how important these social motivators are for collectivistic students, who may be driven more by the desire to help others than to gain personal popularity.

Research suggests that positive interpersonal relationships take on heightened importance for Latino students, particularly their relationships with teachers. Latino students, more than students from other groups, say that a positive and personal relationship with a teacher is important to them (Antrop-González, Vélez, & Garrett, 2003; Nieto, 1998; Valenzuela, 1999). This makes sense, given the view of education/*educación* held by many Latino families. But we are quick to say that it is not only Latino students who benefit from personal relationships in school. A sense of "belongingness" or "connectedness" is fundamental to motivation to learn for students in general (Osterman, 2000; Schaps, 2003).

Most teachers quite likely seek to tap intrinsic motivation—for example, by encouraging students to pursue their own interests when possible through choices of the books they read or projects they do for science or social studies. But we would be surprised to find a teacher who did not attempt to provide *any* extrinsic motivation, whether through the use of rewards, praise, recognition, or the lure of a good grade. Bridging Cultures teachers are no different, but their strategies are distinctly colored by their cultural knowledge of the students they teach.

REWARDS—INDIVIDUAL AND GROUP

Rewards do not appear to be a large part of the classroom repertoire of the Bridging Cultures teachers, but they do use them on occasion. Nevertheless, the rewards take on different forms and meanings, as is made evident by the examples that follow.

Intangible Rewards

One intrinsic reward of engagement in learning activities is the relationship one can have with others, whether through the sense of belonging to a classroom group or through collaboration among a small group of peers. Ms. Altchech discovered that spending time with her, alone or in a small group, was considered a valuable reward by her students. In the following account, she explained her perspective on rewards.

THE BIG REWARD—LUNCH WITH THE TEACHER

First of all, I have never believed, except for an occasional stamp or sticker, in extrinsic rewards. I have never in 25 years of teaching given out rewards. How did this come about? I let them make the decision, and the students said they wanted free time or art [as a reward]. Once I suggested maybe lunch with me [as an option], and the children wanted that above all else. Eventually, they all earned the points to have lunch, so every day I sit with different tables outside during lunch, and I can see their table manners and chit-chat. Now I don't [require] points for any reason; I just enjoy listening to them during lunchtime.

In her approach, Ms. Altchech created a homelike environment by having lunch with the students and in the process was able to gain an understanding of her students' interests and concerns in an informal way. She took something that was essentially a reward for the children and found it to be a reward for herself as well—so much so, in fact, that she stopped requiring that students earn points to have lunch with her. It became a two-way reward—and her action in giving up a quiet, private lunch break says volumes about her priorities.

As this example suggests, the most potent reward may be the teacher's attention and how that is skillfully used as a source of motivation. If given a choice explicitly, would students be more likely to hold up a sign that says "Will Work for a Pizza Party" or "Will Work for Special Time with the Teacher"? Surely, the response would depend upon the caring nature of the teacher (see, for example, Pianta, 2006).

Sharing Rewards Among the Group

When given the option, students will often choose to share a reward, or they find a way that the whole group can be rewarded. Bridging Cultures teachers also reflect the group orientation at times by creating a reward scheme that gives rewards for behavior to the group as a whole rather than to individuals. For example, on some occasions, when Mrs. Hernandez is particularly pleased with how students have been behaving, she puts a small prize in a jar. After the students have earned 20 prizes (or a number equaling the number of students in the class), the prizes are distributed to all members of the class. There is no one-to-one relationship between the "earning" and the distribution of prizes. Students are recognized as a group and rewarded as a group. This treatment of rewards is natural in cultures that consider success to be a group-level phenomenon and that routinely share many forms of property.

We also want to highlight two other relevant examples described more fully in other chapters. In Chapter 4 we described the example of students pooling their fake money, earned for good behavior, to buy a coloring book to share. In Chapter 7, we describe how a star chart, intended to motivate students to attain individual mastery of the times tables, became a tool for documenting progress of an entire 3rd grade classroom toward that goal.

Schoolwide Awards

Although a focus on individual achievement causes discomfort for some students, one cannot assume that students and parents from collectivistic backgrounds will not respond positively to individual awards. Mrs. Hernandez reports that she has found many parents and children motivated by rewards and incentives offered by the school. She noted that she had talked with parent volunteers about one such award. "I told them how the awards worked," she explained. "The easiest award is the attendance award. It is a medal. If they are late to school, no medal. Parents are so psyched about the new awards their children can earn. They don't want their children to miss out because parents *can* ensure that their children are in attendance on their own."

It is significant that in this case it is possible for more than one student to achieve perfect attendance and thus receive an award. Students are not competing for a single award, as they often are when awards such as "Best Writer" or "Top Student" are handed out. Some Bridging Cultures teachers, whenever they have control over awards, insist on a system in which each student (or the whole group) is recognized in some way, so that no one is left out. In an interview, Ms. Saitzyk discussed her feelings about awards assemblies. "Awards assemblies made me uncomfortable," she said, explaining that teachers were required to give specific awards to a few children in categories designated by the school, such as academic achievement, most improved, citizenship, and peer tutoring. She said she became even more uncomfortable after working with the Bridging Cultures framework. "Before, I used to give the assigned number of awards. Then we would have [our own] award ceremony in our class to include everyone. But the year that [I gave] my whole class the awards, I really liked that."

Certainly, in a standards-based system of instruction and grading, there is no reason that many students cannot be recognized for meeting academic standards. However, many students from cultures that emphasize the group may be quite uncomfortable with being singled out for praise in these ways.

PRAISE AND CRITICISM AS MOTIVATORS

Ways of using praise and criticism, with the intention of motivating children in and out of school, are influenced by people's culture-based values. Praise is widely thought to provide "an effective preventative and nonintrusive practice to encourage appropriate behavior . . . [and it has been] associated with increases of appropriate student behavior and task engagement" (Lewis, Newcomer, Trussell, & Richter, 2006, pp. 846–847). Under the assumption that students' self-esteem (1) is important to nourish and (2) will be supported by frequent praise, teachers often praise students—alone and in front of their peers. And the standard wisdom is that teachers, when reporting to parents about their children's progress in school, should "sandwich a small amount of criticism in-between a lot of praise," according to Bridging Cultures teachers' description of the norm. This perception is consonant with what many authorities recommend for how to work with parents (see, for example, Moles, 1996) and is in line with a dominant-culture value of promoting individual achievement and self-esteem.

The recommended approach to praise may not seem genuine to children from collectivistic backgrounds. They may actually mock the teacher's comments of "Beautifully done!" or "Good job" (Geary, 2000; Rothstein-Fisch, 2003). Their parents, who quite likely want to hear what they can do to help their children meet the expectations of the teacher and the school, may be mystified by or uncomfortable with the kind and amount of praise heaped upon their children. We have heard many stories from teachers and graduate students who work with immigrant Latino students that reflect students' and parents' discomfort with praise or even scorn for it.

Tempering praise and evaluating its impact on students and parents is not tantamount to totally eliminating praise in the classroom or during parent-teacher conferences. The meaning, form, and context of praise need to be examined. We have observed that when praise is given privately, so that it does not risk making other students feel left out, it may be more accepted. When students are praised as a group for their accomplishments, they may receive the praise happily. Praising individual students' accomplishments when they are recognized as contributing to a group goal may also be an acceptable approach.

Children reared in a collectivistic culture base their sense of self more on group affiliation than on personal achievement (Markus & Kitayama, 1991). The reverse tends to be true of children reared in an individualistic culture. Although teachers cannot assume how praise or criticism will affect a given student, these guidelines can help teachers to anticipate the kind of information they will need in order to understand the variation in the motivational value of praise or criticism.

An example from Mr. Mercado's class shows how praise can be used effectively. Students were working in collaborative groups to write poems. He pulled the group together for reflection on their work. "This poem has something I like very much. It is the part that is repeated," he said. He read the poem, emphasizing the two repeated phrases. "Why does it sound OK to repeat it?" he asked. Here, Mr. Mercado praised something a group had done and used it as a springboard for discussion of a common feature of poetry, the repetition of words or phrases. Once again, it is the way in which praise is used that needs to be considered if it is to be effective across cultures.

When teachers praise students by saying, "You are so smart," or, "You're great," they are not doing the students any favors; they would do far better to encourage effort. It is important to help students understand that a poor grade is a reflection not of who they are or their innate ability but (nearly always) of their effort. So, although choices about the use of praise need to be made with cultural understanding, teachers also need to factor in what they know more generally about the effects of praise of different types. In fact, focusing on the task performance rather than the individual may make the praise more acceptable to a student from a collectivistic culture who has been taught to be modest.

◆ ◆ ◆ ◆ ◆

We have seen Bridging Cultures teachers use a considerable range of strategies to manage the moment-to-moment flow of classroom activities and personal interactions. Although many of these strategies could readily be applied to almost any classroom, it is evident that cultural knowledge is factored into teachers' choices of strategies. These teachers are obviously aware of using their students' natural inclinations—to cooperate to solve problems, to take responsibility when the teacher is unavailable, and to want to help each other behave appropriately—for positive ends in the classroom.

In some ways, the group orientation and the home value of *respeto* may make the teachers' job in managing the classroom easier. But this is only the case, we believe, when a teacher understands students' home values and can design classroom practices accordingly. Other research has shown that classroom management in the same cultural context as that of the Bridging Cultures classrooms may be time consuming and fraught with conflict when a teacher does not know how to tap cultural resources. For example, in a study comparing a Bridging Cultures 2nd grade class with another 2nd grade class (also composed of Latino immigrant students), Isaac (1999) found that the non-Bridging-Cultures teacher spent an inordinate amount of time regulating students' behavior. Her reprimands often took the form of *discouraging* students from helping each other. Had she known how to capitalize on her students' collaborative and helping skills, she could have greatly increased their time spent on academic tasks.

As a final note, we should say that we and the Bridging Cultures teachers recognize that students sometimes need to work independently. This is a goal of U.S. schooling, and teachers would be doing students no favor by eliminating individual work. However, equipped with cultural knowledge (and tools for acquiring it), teachers can consciously draw on students' skills to foster classroom harmony *and* teach them how to negotiate the expectations of dominant-culture schooling. The notion of orchestration may be useful as educators seek solo and group performances in sync with the students' home and school values.

THE ORGANIZATION OF LEARNING IN THE CONTENT AREAS

A major concern of teachers is organization and management of their language arts programs. Teachers are able with appropriate professional development to integrate cutting-edge strategies into their literacy curriculum, but have a difficult time putting the different pieces of the program together in their school day.

—Lesley M. Morrow, D. Ray Reutzel, and Heather Casey,
"Organization and Management of Language Arts Teaching: Classroom Environments,
Grouping Practices, and Exemplary Instruction," in *Handbook of Classroom Management*

Classroom organization and learning activities are inseparable. In fact, according to Doyle (2006), "the basic unit of classroom organization is the activity" (p. 101). In this chapter, we examine how learning and instructional activities can be organized in ways that are culturally congruent, thus minimizing the need to redirect off-task behavior. We provide an array of examples from Bridging Cultures classrooms to demonstrate how knowledge of the individualism/collectivism framework has shaped instructional activities in language arts and mathematics in particular.

The activity is the fundamental unit of analysis for understanding people's learning in a social context (Cole, Engeström, & Vasquez, 1997; Gutiérrez, 1994; Vygotsky, 1986). Teachers are often encouraged by administrators to specify activity components for each day and to allocate the time required for these activities (Santrock, 2004). "Activities occupy relatively short blocks of classroom time—typically 10 to 20 minutes—during which students are arranged in a particular way . . . [such as] seatwork, recitation, presentations, small groups" (Doyle, 2006, p. 101).

In terms of standard classroom organization, activities can be thought of as having two interrelated dimensions: the *social* and the *physical*. The *social* dimension has to do with how activities and interactions are structured to promote learning and development. It includes the ways language is used; the ways roles and relationships are shaped—in part, through grouping and behavioral expectations; the ways time is allocated and activities sequenced; and the ways students are asked to show what they have learned. Examples presented in earlier chapters highlight the cultural nature of many of these aspects of organization.

The *physical* dimension of organization has to do with how the space and all the materials and equipment of the classroom are structured to promote learning. Of course, the social and physical dimensions are not independent; if teachers want to encourage peer interactions, they may form small groups of tables or push desks together in clusters. In this case, the arrangement of students and furniture could be considered a physical strategy with a social goal (see Doyle, 2006, p. 100). A teacher may "arrange the setting to facilitate traffic flow, communication, supplies and equipment access, private space, and the monitoring of classroom behavior" (Carter & Doyle, 2006, p. 379). Cultural values affect decisions about all of these elements of physical organization. Because we have discussed the physical dimension of classroom organization in Chapter 2, here we focus exclusively on the social dimension.

Bridging Cultures teachers consciously use cultural knowledge to help them organize their instructional activities to maximize student engagement and learning. The strategies we have documented that clearly draw upon cultural knowledge fall into two broad categories: (1) collaborative learning and (2) inclusive discourse (as it relates to how language is used to communicate at home and school). Although the two categories are conceptually distinct, in reality, many of the instructional activities we describe capitalize on both kinds of strategies.

COLLABORATIVE LEARNING

We define *collaborative learning* as "students working together to help each other learn." We prefer the term *collaborative learning* to *cooperative learning* for the following reason. Even though *collaborative* and *cooperative* overlap in their dictionary definitions, the term *cooperative learning* has been associated in the research and practice literature with specific definitions and criteria for implementation, some of which do not apply here (Cohen, 1994; Johnson & Johnson, 1994; Slavin, 1990, 2006). Hollins (1996) describes the distinction as follows:

> In the collaborative learning community, relationships and collaboration among the students are naturally occurring and purposefully focused on learning while minimizing individual and group competition. In contrast, in cooperative learning, relationships are structured, manipulated, and controlled by the teacher with group competition replacing individual competition in many cases. (p. 119)

The kind of working together we are talking about is different from notions of cooperative learning in which each student takes or is assigned a particular role in the group, and individual as well as group grades are awarded. Cooperative learning, as we have observed it in many U.S. classrooms, entails a *task* focus. Students may work quite independently of each other and come together only to plan how to carry out tasks and monitor progress toward completion. In Bridging Cultures classrooms, the *social* and *task* goals are inseparable. In collaborative learning, "the group enforces individual efforts to achieve common goals that represent both social and task-related outcomes" (Wentzel, 2003, p. 324). And, as Sheets (2005) has said, "In collaborative learning groups, interpersonal interactions are at a higher level of personal involvement. Group responsibility is enhanced; participation is more focused on learning and sharing, and the process takes place in a more natural learning context" (p. 156).

A common denominator of the instances of successful collaborative work as we characterize it (and of the most successful forms of cooperative work described elsewhere) is what has been called "positive interdependence" (Johnson, Johnson, & Holubec, 1994). This means that everyone's participation is perceived as contributing to the group's goals, whether the goals are social, academic, or both.

Collaborative learning, in our use of the term, entails genuine working together at a substantive level. As we have typically observed it in Bridging Cultures classrooms, it often involves all students working on all aspects of a task; each student seems to consider it his or her responsibility to solve problems that arise and to ensure that the group accomplishes what is expected of it. When grades are involved, they are often group grades, although teachers make it clear that individual accountability is important as well.

In the remainder of this chapter, we set the scene with a general discussion of the links between collaborative learning and students' home-culture values. Then we turn to the content areas of language arts and mathematics for examples of how collaborative learning takes place in Bridging Cultures classrooms. (Bridging Cultures teachers also use collaborative group work in social studies and science instruction, as well as in other subjects such as physical education, music, and health.)

Cultural Congruence

Small-group collaborative work is a staple of Bridging Cultures classrooms, in part because it is so compatible with students' culture-based strengths. Because working together for the good of the group begins in early childhood within the family, the immigrant Latino students in Bridging Cultures classrooms have well-developed collaborative skills.

Delgado-Gaitan's (1994) research in an immigrant Mexican community in Southern California showed how children taking individual responsibility as early as age 7 expressed itself as responsibility for others—not simply the ability to do things for oneself. Individual capacity is marshaled in support of the group.

There is a natural, *organic* quality (for lack of a better term) to the collaborative learning we have observed in Bridging Cultures classrooms. Students huddle together, planning and discussing as a group. Rarely does a student physically separate from the group to work alone on some aspect of the task; rather, students seem to prefer to work in proximity to each other and to ensure that everyone is included. Although teachers monitor the work of collaborative groups, very little disciplinary intervention is necessary because students have been socialized at home to help each other (notwithstanding their previous experiences in school). Students in Bridging Cultures classrooms need little or no instruction on how to form groups or function in groups (see Chapter 2), and therefore teachers can focus on instructional interventions designed to facilitate high-level cognitive activity.

The collaborative approach applies not only to small-group work but also to large-group and whole-class activities, a fact that becomes clear in the classroom examples that follow. The elements of collaboration may not be immediately apparent, however. At times they are more in the nature of students' orientation to each other's achievement; an activity that actually promotes competition in individualistic settings can engender cooperation in a collectivistic group.

Collaborating in Language Arts

Bridging Cultures teachers have described many strategies to maximize collaboration in language arts instruction. These strategies can be applied across a wide range of grade levels, with minor adaptations. As mentioned, collaboration and certain forms of cooperative learning have been shown to have positive academic, personal, and interpersonal impact (Atwell, 1987; Gambrell, Mazzoni, & Almasi, 2000; Johnson & Johnson, 1994).

Vocabulary pairs. Mrs. Pérez allows students to help each other study vocabulary. Students with greater English proficiency help those with lesser proficiency, though "proficiency" is not a consistently predictable state. Sometimes it is the "less proficient" student who is seen to be explaining something to a "more proficient" student because he or she has certain expertise. This kind of heterogeneous grouping is reflective of Mrs. Pérez's beliefs about what helps students learn, and it parallels the pattern of older siblings helping younger ones in many collectivistic families (Delgado-Gaitan, 1994; Maynard, 2002; Nsamenang & Lamb, 1994). She avoids ability grouping in general, seeking activities in which students can learn from each other. She believes that those who serve as tutors for their peers also benefit from making their own knowledge explicit. Her beliefs are born out by research (see Antil, Jenkins, & Wayne, 1998).

Group writing. All Bridging Cultures teachers use some form of "process writing" instruction, in which students go through steps of brainstorming, drafting pieces of writing, and engaging in peer review and editing (Calkins, 1983). At one of our Bridging Cultures meetings, Ms. Altchech said, "I go one step further. Many students aren't 'there' for writing in English, so teams are writing stories together. . . . Students can choose to write individually and illustrate and type together. For assessment, I have them alternate so I can see individual performance." But, she noted, "they do not always write in a group. I have done scripted poetry, journal writing, and other [kinds of] individual writing."

Class books. In this activity, individual work leads to a group product that is shared by the whole class. Mrs. Pérez had children create posters about themselves on 11-by-17-inch paper as a homework assignment. When the students brought their creations to class, she interviewed each child, and the children learned about each other. "The collectivistic part is putting [the posters] together as a class book," she said, citing this activity as an example of how the individualism/collectivism framework had transformed what she did in the classroom.

Mrs. Pérez laminated the pages so that they would stand up to ongoing handling by more than 20 students, who appeared to take great pride in their joint product. By joining their narratives, they created a book that they could all read. In this case, the support for group learning came after the original activity, but the seeds of collaboration were there.

On another occasion, she paired her 3rd graders with 1st graders, with whom they had a buddy arrangement. They were to collaborate on a single book based on a story they had heard called *If*. Mrs. Pérez described what happened:

> They drew on paper and cut out their drawings. They wrote a sentence on the computer—some in English, some in Spanish. Some of their pages illustrated things like "If people could smell wind . . . ," "If tables could have faces . . . ," "If grass could be eyebrows . . . ," "If my heart were a butterfly . . . ," "If a whale could run in the park . . . ," "If apples could eat trees . . . ." Reading the whole finished product as a group, they were in awe of each other's work.

Ms. Altchech described a similar experience, in which an individual writing activity culminated in a group product. After a field trip, Ms. Altchech's students wrote thank-you notes to the Audubon Society. The notes were gathered into a book and sent to the docents who had helped the class learn about the wetlands they visited.

Choral reading. Choral reading refers to children reading aloud as a group. Bridging Cultures teachers recommend this practice as well as individual reading as a regular part of daily language arts instruction. One particular benefit of choral reading is that it allows students with limited English proficiency to practice the rhythm and sound of English without being spotlighted, and thus it is compatible with the collectivist value of not standing out.

Mr. Mercado uses a variation on choral reading called "popcorn." He has modified what was originally designed as an individual reading activity and uses it with pairs. Sitting with two children at a table, he reads a little, and then taps the table to signal the children to begin reading chorally. He reports that "popcorn" and choral reading are popular even with children who are normally hesitant to read aloud.

Extending the choral approach to other aspects of the classroom, teachers may allow children to answer chorally instead of individually. Choral reading and choral response have been shown to be successful in such different environments as Alaska native villages, native Hawaiian communities, and other Pacific Island communities, all of which share similar norms of collaboration (Au & Jordan, 1981; Lipka et al., 1998; Nelson-Barber, Trumbull, & Wenn, 2000).

Literature circles. In literature circles, small groups of students discuss the same piece of literature, asking each other questions and critically analyzing various facets of the reading. Literature circles have been shown to increase students' engagement in reading and to expand their understanding of texts (Daniels, 2002; Fox &Wilkinson, 1997; Noll, 1994). Fall, Webb, & Chudowsky (2000) found that 10th grade students who were allowed to have a 10-minute collaborative discussion about a story they had read before taking a 90-minute test demonstrated significantly greater comprehension than peers who had not participated in such discussions.

In Ms. Altchech's classroom, each group that makes up a circle selects its own literature to read, and each student has a particular responsibility that benefits the whole group. These circles help develop vocabulary, reading fluency, comprehension, oral language, and critical interpretation, according to Ms. Altchech. Each reading of a piece of literature leads to a "benchmark"—some form of presentation of the book to the rest of the class. "The scores depend upon the collaborative group," she explained. "They love it. . . . They do the work together and do the tasks together." The groups are heterogeneous in terms of reading ability. "[Students] help the ones in the group that have more problems," Ms. Altchech said.

Unleveled drama activities. Mrs. Pérez's 3rd grade students tend to be at three levels of reading proficiency: 1st, 2nd, and 3rd grade. She uses drama as a way to get the children involved in literacy activities in which they can all participate and that do not require that they be at the same level of proficiency. The students work with partners to read together and learn their parts for the drama. They make costumes and invite others to attend the performance. The activity promotes "a group feeling" and "draws on collectivistic values," Mrs. Pérez said. "No one [knows] who [is] a 1st-grade-level or 3rd-grade-level reader. . . . All students are the same age. [The less proficient readers] aren't behind socially." She said the activity has empowered groups to move to the next level in reading ability.

Whole-group Zoo Phonics. Ms. Daley's 2nd grade uses a commercial program called "Zoo Phonics" that relies heavily on kinesthetic and visual cues to help students make sound-letter associations. Each letter-sound has an associated story, and each letter has an associated character, such as Ellie Elephant or Ana Ardilla (*ardilla* is the Spanish word for "squirrel"). "The characters motivate the children," Ms. Daley explained. "For Ana Ardilla, every time she wants to crack a nut, she slaps her fist into her paw; the kids imitate the movement and associate the sound . . . All [of the characters] have personalities, and all mean something." Ms. Daley reported that the program is effective for Latino children "because it's so group-oriented. They chant in unison, do the movements together, and remember it easily."

Collaborating in Mathematics

Historically, math practice has involved considerable independent study. Students may prepare flash cards, practice alone, and test themselves for accuracy. Preparing for timed tests of math facts is often a form of drudgery for students, who have to rehearse in isolation until they are ready for testing. The process of solitary studying and self-testing may seem like a good idea to teachers who work with children of immigrant parents. Teachers may assume that parents have limited time and perhaps do not have the skills necessary to guide homework practice. They may also reason that the more independent the children can become in studying, the more likely they are to become successful students. However, this individualistic approach may seriously undercut the power of the group—both in homework and in classroom-based learning. Although students must attain automaticity with basic math facts, there is no reason that this goal cannot be met through a group orientation.

Mastering math facts. Mrs. Pérez was observed applying her knowledge of both collectivistic and individualistic values to develop a number of group-based activities to improve math skills. She draws upon students' inclination to help each other *and* promotes individual mastery of math facts through several strategies. In the activity described here, even when the emphasis is on individual mastery of facts, a group process supports such mastery.

MATH FACT "FRIENDS"

The students had each produced a set of cards with math facts (addition, subtraction, multiplication, division), which they kept in small plastic zipped bags. At the beginning of the day, Mrs. Pérez asked the students to select one fact from their bag and study it from time to time throughout the day— specifically, to look at it, think about it, practice it, and then put it away. Mrs. Pérez suggested that this fact card was like their "math friend" for the day.

Immediately following morning recess, Mrs. Pérez instructed the students to sit on the rug. She asked each student to hold up his or her fact that had been chosen as the "math friend" of the day (e.g., $4 + 3 = 7$). With very little direction from the teacher, one student came to the front of the class to lead the others in demonstrating knowledge of their math facts.

As the student began to lead the group, Mrs. Pérez moved to her desk nearby to work on some papers. The student leader began calling on fellow students, one at a time, to share their memorized math fact. Once selected, each volunteer came to the front of the class, handed the math fact to the self-appointed class leader, and recited the math fact by heart, as the student leader checked for accuracy. If a student did not remember the fact correctly, the leader gave the card back as a prompt. When the fact was recited correctly, the leader offered the student a plush toy with a pull-string that, when stretched and released, created a vibration. As soon as the vibration stopped, the student handed it back to the student leader, and the next student was called on for recitation of a new math fact. This activity lasted until all the children who wanted to share their fact had a turn, for a total duration of about 15 minutes.

Students were remarkably attentive and focused respectfully on each fellow student's presentation of a fact. There was no disruptive behavior and no evidence of boredom or lack of interest on the part of the students.

Later, in a conversation with the observer, Mrs. Pérez noted that typically an elected class officer "leads the math activity, but this time another child self-selected. She just took the leadership role, and the children are so used to sharing the leadership that it doesn't matter who leads. They just figure it out. They also decide when to stop." In other classrooms, children might be inclined to become tired of an activity like this if it wasn't "their turn," but with these students and this teacher, this was not the case. Why?

First, it is likely that children were taught to be respectful by their parents and families, and they demonstrated what they had learned by respecting each other in the classroom. The observation occurred in the third month of the school year, so it is likely that ample time had been spent on establishing a classroom setting that supported respectfulness.

Second, students were able to get support when needed, because they could get their math fact back if they needed to prompt their memory. The opportunity for a second chance led to success for each student, but because of the atmosphere of respect and support, there was no real risk of shame or embarrassment if a student did not remember the fact. Despite the expectation for individual performance, the activity was not framed as a competition. There was no apparent tension, as there often is when students are explicitly or implicitly pitted against each other (see Isaac, 1999).

Third, using the vibrating toy seemed like a clever way to put some fun into the learning experience. The brief action of pulling the string to make the toy vibrate wasn't belabored, and no students asked for extra turns. They knew that one answer led to exactly one turn with the toy, and they seemed to feel satisfied, whether they remembered the fact or had to use a prompt to get the right answer. Each student's engagement with the toy appeared to bring vicarious pleasure to the onlookers.

Fourth, the activity encouraged both individual and group orientations to learning. Each student had to demonstrate learning but had the support of the group to do so. The group could also practice the fact along with the student. For example, if the student recited (or read) the fact "nine minus four equals . . . ," then the children could be thinking about their answer along with the student at the front of the class. It could also be argued that Mrs. Pérez's casting of the math fact card as a "friend" was an effort to recognize students' valuing of social relationships.

Math teams. An account by Mrs. Hernandez shows how students transform an apparently competitive, individualistic activity into a collaborative one:

> I make two rows of students, and, depending upon their level, I have two sets of flashcards. They score a point for their team if they can read the flashcard. It is not competition but helping your team get a point. They really encourage each other. They say, "You can do it!" Even the kids from the other team cheer on their friends. [Students] clap for the winning teams. [There are] no real [extrinsic] rewards.

This simple example is a powerful demonstration of how events are interpreted through a cultural lens. The students do not construe the activity as necessarily competitive, and because Mrs. Hernandez understands her students and their values, she does not force it into a competitive frame. Here, collaboration is not overtly structured in the activity, but it takes place naturally.

The following example from Mrs. Pérez's class illustrates another instance of group support.

EXPLORING THE CONCEPT OF 1,000

The children in Mrs. Pérez's class were studying the concept of "1,000." She began the lesson by constructing a number line on the white board: 10 < 100 < 1,000 < 10,000. She asked the class to remember what the "less than" symbol (<) meant. Organized into tables of four children each, the groups were charged with collecting 1,000 items. Each group had to decide what to collect. But how were they going to collect 1,000 objects? Mrs. Pérez asked the students how they could help other tables. Ten children responded, saying things such as, "I can bring pennies to help Table 3"; "I can bring in rocks"; "I can bring in plastic bags." Other items the students planned to gather included nails, marbles, and crayons. When Mrs. Pérez asked them what they were going to do next, the children said, "Get our stuff out, help each other, and count." In her instructions, she reminded students that "the most important thing is to work together." While the groups collaborated, Mrs. Pérez selected children individually to be tested on their multiplication facts.

Students worked together to decide how to group their objects for counting. One group decided to group by 100s, but as they began counting, they realized that they were having problems remembering how many they had counted out. They discussed what would be the best number for each grouping of objects, settling on 25. Other groups used groupings of 10, 20, 50, and 100.

During a debriefing following the group work, the groups reported on how many objects they had gathered and how many more they needed. They also described the method they used to count their objects. This activity let other students know how many more pennies, rocks, or nails to gather (identifying which group needed the most help), while allowing the children to see the many different ways that objects could be grouped. Discussion centered on why certain objects were easier to count in larger or smaller groups, making explicit the strategies behind the choices the children had made. For instance, children counting pennies made stacks of 10 pennies each and could check their work or accuracy by looking at the height of the stacks.

In learning about the concept of 1,000, the children worked in small groups and then as a whole group, without the kind of competition that one might see if the teacher had set up a classroom contest to see which student could collect his or her own objects first, or which small group could complete the task first. When asked about the lesson during a short interview following this observation, Mrs. Pérez said she uses "the power [of the group] to let go and trust the collective result."

There was no reward for "the first group to get to 1,000" but rather a sense of shared accomplishment and helping. Teachers who think that they need to provide incentives such as a reward for success in a competition may be undermining the possibility of students' engaging in a much more collaborative experience that helps each group succeed.

INCLUSIVE DISCOURSE

An important social aspect of classroom organization involves the ways that linguistic communication—referred to as *classroom discourse* (Cazden, 2001; Morine-Dershimer, 2006)—is carried out. Of course, *discourse* (communication of thought through words) is part of all of the activities described in the earlier section on collaboration, but here we present examples explicitly focused on discourse.

Inclusive discourse refers to the practice of incorporating students' home-grown ways of using language in instruction and the life of the classroom. Most classrooms have rules about who can talk when, about what, and in what manner, and predictable communication routines are established early in the school year (Morine-Dershimer, 2006). We have found that Bridging Cultures teachers create learning environments that not only tolerate but encourage the discourse styles based on the students' home culture. The ability to participate in the discourse of the classroom is important not only because teachers often evaluate and grade students on participation but also because students apparently learn more when they participate verbally (Morine-Dershimer, 2006). "A good classroom manager working with primary grade minority children may spend extra time directly teaching the rules and routines pertaining to traditional classroom communication and greatly improve student achievement as a result" (Morine-Dershimer, 1985, cited in Morine-Dershimer, 2006, p. 133). But teachers need to recognize that differences in students' discourse do not necessarily signal deficiencies in language development or learning ability. They also need to acknowledge that home discourse does not need to be displaced by new discourse.

Valuing Students' Ways with Words

The phrase "ways with words," which we purposefully use in the heading for this section, evokes Heath's (1983) book of the same name based on her ethnographic study of several speech communities in the Piedmont Carolinas. The term incorporates not only the actual vocabulary and syntax used by a particular group, but also the purposes (intellectual, social, religious, and other) language is used for; how conversation, stories, and formal talk are structured; how topics are chosen, maintained, and changed; and more.

In addition to the turn-taking aspect of discourse, the matters of how topics are selected, introduced, and developed in conversation have a cultural foundation and need to be examined. Teachers generally have particular expectations for how students should participate in discussions about science or social studies, mathematics or literature. Whether it is made explicit or not, the expectation is usually that academic knowledge is treated as something separate from one's personal experience. A question such as, "What have you learned about the desert?" is not intended, ordinarily, to elicit tales of family outings. The teacher is looking for logical-scientific thinking and the appropriate discourse to express it, not a narrative incorporating social experience (Bruner, 1996).

These two types of discourse—logical-scientific and social narrative—differ in content and vocabulary, and they also are structured quite differently. The following example illustrates what can happen when a young child responds with a social narrative when the teacher is trying to elicit early logical-scientific discourse. Note that the teacher's question appears to call for a social narrative, yet some children correctly understand her to be calling for logical-scientific discourse.

DESCRIBING AN EGG

During one of our observations of a Los Angeles prekindergarten class made up of mostly Latino children, the teacher was showing a real chicken egg that would soon hatch. . . She asked children to describe the eggs by thinking about the times they had cooked and eaten them. One child tried three times to talk about how she had cooked eggs with her grandmother, but the teacher disregarded these comments in favor of a child who explained that the insides of eggs are white and yellow. A Latina member of our research team noted that the first child's answer was typical of the associations that her invisible home culture encourages. That is, objects are most meaningful when they mediate social interactions. But in this case, the teacher expected students to describe eggs as isolated physical entities. Eggs as mediators of social relationships and social behavior were irrelevant. (Trumbull, Greenfield, & Quiroz, 2003, p. 75, based on Greenfield, Raeff, & Quiroz, 1996)

Bridging Between Stories and Academic Discourse

The Bridging Cultures teachers reported that their students love to tell stories, particularly about their experiences with their families. All of the teachers consciously encouraged children's stories for self-expression, for tapping prior knowledge, and for bridging to classroom discourse. Stories nearly always involve family members and reflect the importance of integrating the social dimension of life with the "cognitive" or "academic." It is important to emphasize that in the case of Bridging Cultures teachers' instruction, inclusion of children's stories was not just an entrée to classroom discourse but was perceived as an opportunity to acknowledge other forms of discourse as valid in their own right. The inclusion was also a recognition of the values underlying the discourse. This personal kind of discourse is valued and natural to many students, particularly from collectivistic cultures (Martinez-Roldan & Lopez-Robertson, 2000, cited in Chen, 2006; Trumbull, Rothstein-Fisch, et al., 2000).

The T-chart. Elsewhere we have written about how Ms. Altchech consciously showed her students how to bridge from their story-based, narrative knowledge to what might be termed "scientific discourse" (Rothstein-Fisch, 2003; Trumbull, Diaz-Meza, & Hasan, 2000). As part of Ms. Altchech's class's preparation for a field trip to some local wetlands, a docent from the Audubon Society was visiting the classroom. He asked the students what they knew about birds of the wetlands, and many students offered personal stories of birds they had seen, usually with family members. Stories of family trips and interactions with grandmothers and aunties abounded. Frustrated, the docent admonished the students, "No more stories!" Of course, his next question was met with dead silence. Ms. Altchech remembered the story of the egg, discussed at one of the Bridging Cultures meetings.

After he left, Ms. Altchech tried to pick up the pieces of the discussion. She drew a T-chart on the board, writing in key phrases from students' stories on the left side and coaching them to extract the "scientific information" for the right side of the chart (see Figure 6.1).

On reflection, Ms. Altchech noted that even before taking part in the Bridging Cultures Project she had "always tapped children's prior knowledge—social or cognitive. What is new, though, after the Audubon experience, was how to get to the science information. The development of the T-chart . . . I wanted them to see the connection."

Teachers can tap students' culture-based ways of knowing and talking *and* introduce them to new forms of discourse, as we see in the T-chart example. Why should a single way of communicating, learning, and interacting dominate in the classroom, particularly when students bring a different set of skills to that context? The examples show that there are ways to organize classroom interaction that differ from the ones we often take for granted. By using the T-chart, Ms.

Altchech created a sort of hybrid discourse, which incorporated features of both students' and traditional discourse (Gutiérrez, Baquedano-López, & Tejeda, 1999).

FIGURE 6.1

Bridging Stories with Science Information

Student Experience	Scientific Information
I was playing in the garden with my grandmother. I saw a hummingbird near the cherry tree. It was really pretty. The bird stood in the air. I tried to go close to the little bird, but it kept darting away.	Hummingbird • Bird is brownish with bright iridescent green and red coloring around head and neck. • Wings beat rapidly. • Bird can hover and fly in any direction. • Has to eat frequently because of using so much energy in its movements (high metabolism).

Source: From *Bridging Cultures Teacher Education Module*, by C. Rothstein-Fisch, 2003, Mahwah, NJ: Lawrence Erlbaum Associates. Adapted with permission.

Expanding Opportunities to Participate in Different Kinds of Discourse

Mrs. Hernandez discussed how the Bridging Cultures Project affected her approach to classroom organization by promoting new forms of discourse: "The class *was* organized by ability groups; *now* the whole group gets support from each other." According to Mrs. Hernandez, this allows her to "free up her sense of control," both with children (now used as collaborators) and parents (used as classroom volunteers). Commenting on the importance of having children talk more, she said, "Children need to communicate at school because they don't get this at home." She went on to discuss how, in the home setting, where the cultural value of respect for elders may prevail, children are not necessarily encouraged to engage in either public speaking or in exchanges with adults. Mrs. Hernandez is consciously attempting to use organizational structures that promote students' engagement in forms of discourse that they do not use at home. One such structure, heterogeneous grouping, has been shown to support wider participation of previously quiet students (Antil, Jenkins, & Wayne, 1998; Cohen, 1994). Mrs. Hernandez believes strongly that her students need to acquire new ways of using language in addition to the ones they have learned at home, if they want to succeed in school and in life in the United States.

THE CONTENT OF DISCOURSE

Closely related to the organization of discourse in the classroom is the *content* of discourse. Personal experience and family-related themes can serve as an important source of content for students from collectivistic cultures.

Family Experience

It is not uncommon for Bridging Cultures teachers to make efforts to link instruction to students' personal experience, and sometimes to their own, in order to make instruction more meaningful. This strategy of connecting with what students already know is compatible with constructivist notions of learning (Bransford, Brown, & Cocking, 2000). With students who consider the personal and social aspects of life to be a natural part of academic life, this strategy becomes all the more important. In fact, Bridging Cultures teachers routinely use students' experiences as a basis for instruction. The personal becomes part of the discourse of the classroom—not something relegated to portions of circle time or recess. For example, mathematics word problems are likely to be about real or hypothetical family experiences (a trip to Mexico, shopping for a holiday dinner), or about an experience the class has shared (a field trip, planning a class party). The following excerpt from an observation in Mr. Mercado's classroom depicts him trying to get his students to think about how to solve a cost-pricing problem in a context they know.

HOW TO PRICE TAMALES

Mr. M: You are going to sell tamales with your mom. You make special tamales ... What do you use to make them?

Students: Meat, masa [corn meal], chili, bread, peppers, and banana leaves.

Mr. M: How much will you sell them for?

Students: Two dollars.

Mr. M: How much does it cost to make them?

Students: Three dollars.

Mr. M: Is it too expensive to make tamales?

Students: Cut them in half ... Raise the price of the tamales ... Use less breadmeal.

In addition to providing a meaningful way for students to consider a mathematical situation, incorporating tamales into the lesson was interesting because the children mentioned distinctly different tamale ingredients, depending upon their families' region of origin. They seemed proud to say what their families' tamales would be made of, but they quickly returned to the primary idea of how to make cost-effective tamales. Without this knowledge or interest, the teacher might have constructed the word problem around something completely foreign to the students. Instead, he used his cultural knowledge to situate the problem in a meaningful context.

Sometimes personalizing instruction can entail teachers sharing their own experiences as well as drawing upon students' experiences. For example, Ms. Daley taught her students about the moon and the vocabulary word *crescent* by telling them about how, as a little girl, she went with her grandmother to the bakery to get a crescent roll. The students could remember the concept and the word by recalling Ms. Daley's account of her trips to the bakery.

Family-Related Themes

Social studies curriculum in the elementary grades often relates to the local community. Mr. Mercado, teaching 4th grade, has consciously made more links to students' most immediate community —their family. The stories and bulletin board display about grandmothers described in Chapter 2 is one example. Another unit that Mr. Mercado used required students to conduct interviews with family members about family traditions, foods, and activities; construct genealogies; and create anthologies of family stories. Mr. Mercado said that using a writing prompt incorporating something the children are knowledgeable about motivates students to be "more involved and more on task." A corollary benefit is good behavior: "If a child is more interested, there are naturally less problems. That leads to good classroom management and good cooperation."

In another example of using family themes, Mrs. Hernandez recognized the importance of a student's family-oriented discourse.

GRANDMOTHER'S CLOCK

I [try] to listen to everybody and not discourage them from relating family experiences as they relate to the concepts being taught. I started to teach "time" this week, and one of the kindergartners raised her hand and said, "We bought a clock for my grandmother's room, and her name is Magdalena." And then she became much more interested in the clock and everything since she could say her grandmother's name with pride. (Trumbull, Diaz-Meza, Hasan, & Rothstein-Fisch, 2001, p. 26)

◆ ◆ ◆ ◆ ◆

It is clear that there are many ways to bring students' culture-based strengths into the classroom. We have seen how Bridging Cultures teachers choose strategies in grouping, structures for participation, and use of discourse to promote student engagement, thus minimizing the need to use classroom management strategies such as redirection or behavioral reinforcement. When students are engaged, teachers spend less time reprimanding them for being off task.

Of course, many of the practices we have described are used in classrooms of all kinds, but what may distinguish Bridging Cultures classrooms is the depth and breadth of such practices and the consciousness with which teachers engage in them. These teachers continue to invent new ways of aligning classroom norms with those of students' homes *and* of introducing new forms of participation so that students will be successful in school.

In Chapter 7, we take on the question of how assessment practices are related to classroom orchestration, and how there, too, culture plays an important role. We explore both formal and informal assessment and then turn our attention to issues of what constitutes helping versus cheating.

CLASSROOM ORCHESTRATION
OF THE ASSESSMENT PROCESS

Teachers who understand how . . . culture must be considered in assessments can play a strong role in ensuring that assessment practices are more fair, valid, and ethical.

—Elise Trumbull and Maria Pacheco,
The Teacher's Guide to Diversity: Building a Knowledge Base

Classroom orchestration is as much a part of the assessment process as it is of other aspects of instruction. Thus culture is implicated in the ways assessment is designed and carried out. In this chapter, we show how Bridging Cultures teachers have incorporated a group orientation in their assessment practices, with positive results for their students. Their innovations reflect an understanding that it is not just the content and language of assessment that need to be considered to make assessment culturally appropriate for students but also the processes surrounding assessment itself (Abedi, Leon, & Mirocha, 2001; August & Hakuta, 1997; Durán, 1985; Solano-Flores & Trumbull, 2003; Valdés & Figueroa, 1994). We describe how teachers harnessed the value that students place on helping and on group

Authors' note: This chapter is adapted from "When 'Helping Someone Else' Is the Right Answer: Bridging Cultures in Assessment," by Carrie Rothstein-Fisch, Elise Trumbull, Adrienne Isaac, Catherine Daley, and Amada Irma Pérez, 2003, *Journal of Latinos and Education*, 2(3), pp. 123–140. Copyright 2003 by Lawrence Erlbaum Associates, Inc. All rights reserved. Adapted with permission.

success to prepare them for standardized tests and to promote "test wiseness." We show how teachers have made both assessment and the grading process sensible to students, as well as how they have helped students distinguish between *helping* and *cheating*—not a trivial concern when assessment crosses cultures.

THE NATURE OF ASSESSMENT IN U.S. CLASSROOMS

Assessment is usually a lonely enterprise in U.S. classrooms, with students expected to demonstrate what they have learned without assistance from others. Assessment may take many forms, including (1) questioning during discussions (assessment embedded in instruction); (2) teacher-constructed activities (such as weekly tests, oral presentations, or written assignments); (3) publishers' end-of-unit tests; or (4) large-scale standardized tests. Sometimes alternative methods such as portfolios or exhibitions in front of a panel of judges are used. Tacit assumptions about how these forms of assessment should be carried out and how students should participate in them underlie teachers' approaches to all types of assessment.

These assumptions are situated in a particular cultural perspective. For instance, a teacher from the dominant U.S. culture (or one educated in U.S. schools) may expect that when she asks a question as an informal index of student learning, only one student should reply at a time. A student from a group-oriented culture may assume no such thing and find it awkward to be singled out to respond individually; it may also seem unnatural to students to refrain from helping each other (see Chapter 4).

Classroom assessment and large-scale formal testing are frequent and ongoing in U.S. classrooms (see Popham, 2003; Stiggins, 1997). Teachers complain about the amount of time spent on mandated district and state testing (Ohanian, 2001; Popham, 2003), which has increased since the passage of the No Child Left Behind Act in 2001. In particular, large-scale testing has implications for classroom organization and orchestration because it is separate from instruction and must be carried out in ways that may not parallel classroom approaches to assessment. This discontinuity potentially affects all students; however, it may have an even greater impact on students from nondominant cultures who may have less experience with decontextualized examination of their knowledge and learning (see, for example, Beaumont, de Valenzuela, & Trumbull, 2002; Farr & Trumbull, 1997). In other words, students from collectivistic cultures may have an especially hard time with concepts that do not have any connection to something familiar or are not presented within a social context.

Practices that reduce the discontinuity between students' experiences and the approach to assessment stand to improve the assessment process and likely the outcome as well. Bridging Cultures teachers and their students designed many such practices.

PREPARATION FOR TESTING

In this section, we explore how two Bridging Cultures teachers used their students' cultural strengths to prepare for or participate in various types of assessment. We look at examples in three contexts: informal classroom assessment, formal classroom assessment linked to grade-level standards, and standardized assessment.

Helping in the Context of Informal Assessment

The following examples illustrate different reactions to the same behavior during informal assessment activities in two classrooms. The first example is from the 2nd grade classroom of a teacher who is not part of the Bridging Cultures Project; the second example is from Mrs. Pérez's classroom.

In the first classroom, the teacher was conducting a discussion and calling on students for answers to her questions. The children were whispering answers among themselves after one student was called on to respond to the teacher. The teacher said, "I have heard people whispering, and I really don't like it, because why? They need to learn by themselves, and you really aren't helping them learn." (See Isaac, 1999, p. 34.)

In this example, the teacher took the individualistic perspective that children need to "learn by themselves." By whispering (a practice the children would perceive as helping their friends), they were, in the teacher's mind, interfering with their own learning as well as that of their peers. Moreover, the teacher chastised the children directly, stating "I don't like it" and quite likely undermining their belief that helping others is a valuable thing to do. Her stance put the children in the position of having to choose (consciously or unconsciously) between a value of home and a value of school.

In contrast, an observation in Mrs. Pérez's class revealed a different take on whispering. Seven 3rd grade students were sitting on the rug, discussing the material they had just read. Mrs. Pérez noticed that one child seemed to be answering most of the questions. She encouraged him to "whisper the answer to a friend" so that the other child could answer. According to Mrs. Pérez, this practice "lets both children feel successful and work cooperatively." Her knowledge of the collectivistic orientation of her students allowed her to take a different view of peers helping each other. Thus, Mrs. Pérez not only sanctioned whispering, she actively encouraged it as a means of helping others.

Helping in the Context of Formal Assessment Linked to Grade-Level Standards

A Bridging Cultures example. This example of modification to the assessment process shows how children's group orientation and eagerness to help can result in improved math performance relative to grade-level standards. On a visit to Mrs. Pérez's classroom, the observer noticed a "star chart" displaying children's names and corresponding stars next to them, indicating the level of memorized multiplication facts they had mastered. The star chart was a curious object of individual achievement in an otherwise group-oriented classroom, and the teacher was asked about her rationale for using it. Mrs. Pérez responded:

For many years I had known about having charts where children's names are up, and they collect stars when they pass different things, especially . . . in math. I had tried using them as a new and young teacher, but I always felt bad because it just seemed like the children who didn't do well would feel really bad because they would not have as many stars as the other ones. So I felt the emphasis was on failure rather than success. I went ahead and tried it, but I was never happy with it . . . For a while, I put it on the inside of the closet door. It was a struggle for me, but I didn't know why.

Mrs. Pérez's original use of the star chart seems to reflect a typical motivational practice, anchored to beliefs about the need to support individual achievement. Mrs. Pérez continued to describe her experience:

As time passed, I just quit using the charts completely. Then years passed, and I went to Bridging Cultures meetings. I started learning another way of thinking, and I started learning about the success of groups collectively. Something clicked inside of me, and I decided that I still had children that needed to learn their multiplication tables, so I decided to try bringing it out again, to use the power of the group to help everybody succeed.

So I posed the question to the students in a class meeting; we all looked at the chart together and talked about it. The students said, "Wouldn't it be neat if it would be a solid block of stars, and the whole chart was filled in?" and everybody said, "Yeah, yeah, that would be so neat." The students . . . wanted to help each other. Everyone who needed help got adopted by students who had already mastered [the work]. They started helping each other pass, and they seemed to move ahead. The buddies put their own learning on hold in order to help their buddies, not for individual success, but for the success of the group.

The star chart didn't "click" for Mrs. Pérez until it was reconceptualized as a tool for reflecting the achievement of the class as a whole. Achievement was not about acquiring a star for any particular child (which might, in collectivistic terms, make the child uncomfortable about standing out from the whole group). Rather, each star would be an important contribution to the whole—filling in part of the entire grid to reflect the group's progress. The children, empowered by their own tendency to think and act collectively, were highly motivated to achieve group success. And the new star chart strategy allowed them to act on the cultural value of helping others. Mrs. Pérez noticed that the buddies watched vigilantly as their partners were tested:

> When [the children] felt that they were ready and the buddy was confident that they were ready for the oral timed test with the teacher, [they would come up for testing]. According to the order in which they signed up, I would call them up, and they were allowed to bring their buddy up for moral support. While the buddy watched—and they weren't allowed to say anything—the person being tested experienced success most of the time. If they were successful, they would ring a bell and receive applause from everyone. (Rothstein-Fisch, Trumbull, Isaac, Daley, & Pérez, 2003, pp. 132–134)

In this case, students' buddies not only promoted memorization of multiplication facts, they also played a role in the assessment process. When the student achieved success—demonstrating mastery of a new level of timed math facts—he or she would ring a bell. The bell was a signal to the whole class that another star was being added to *their* group chart. For a moment, students stopped working to recognize and applaud the achievement of their classmates—both the student who had achieved the next level of math accomplishment and the buddy who had helped. This procedure did not single out the student being tested but rather highlighted the team that worked together for the benefit of the whole group. Without any disruption, the students clapped and then immediately returned to their work. This same process was observed on several occasions. According to Mrs. Pérez,

> If they were not successful, then they felt bad, but their buddy was right there with them, [saying,] "We'll work more and I'll help you." [The buddies] gave them so much confidence to help them again. They would go back and practice more and in different ways until they were ready to take the test again. They never got discouraged because they had their buddy. Eventually they passed. This went on until we achieved 100 percent up to a certain point. The kids were ecstatic. They achieved a whole block of stars! [It was] a day of celebration. They were even more encouraged to go on. In 3rd grade, they only have to go up to the 5s [tables], but many went to the 12s! All got to the 6s . . . They went beyond the requirement. It was extremely exciting.

Reflecting months later, Mrs. Pérez commented, "How could I have not done that all these years? I didn't have the clear knowledge of the framework of individualism and collectivism. I continue to use that" (Rothstein-Fisch et al., 2003, pp. 133–134).

A non-Bridging Cultures example. The use of math "teams" in a non–Bridging Cultures classroom provides a contrasting example and shows how what appears to be a collaborative learning activity can be, in fact, highly individualized and competitive. In a videotaped observation of a math assessment activity in a classroom composed mainly of immigrant Latino students, Isaac (1999) recorded one such activity:

> The classroom was divided into two groups, and a representative from each group came up to the board to answer the same addition problem. Even though the class was organized into two groups, the students were not allowed to help their teammates. As each student representative approached the board,

the children shouted, "Ooooh," indicative of the pressure this activity evoked. Some of the children even positioned themselves as if praying. The two children at the board were actually competing with each other without any help or support from their group members.

Isaac reports that the children showed signs of great stress. What a difference compared to the students in Mrs. Pérez's class!

Helping in the Context of Standardized Assessment

Testing has become an increasingly important factor in high-stakes decision making in education (Ercikan, 2006), and Bridging Cultures teachers, like other teachers, spend time preparing their students for standardized assessments. But test preparation in Bridging Cultures classrooms may seem quite different from traditional preparation. Mrs. Pérez and Ms. Daley have capitalized on their students' culture-based value of helping as they prepare their classes for standardized tests.

Test prep in Mrs. Pérez's class. Here is how Mrs. Pérez articulated her experiences with helping students prepare for standardized tests:

I also use a lot of collectivistic activities to prepare the students for individual, standardized testing. When we practice multiple-choice tests . . . all the children take the tests individually in silence, with privacy screens. They take their tests, and then we correct them in a group, orally. Each table or cooperative group is responsible for one question. So they can discuss it together . . . what the best answer is. Then all the members of the table stand, and everyone has a role. Person #1 reads the question; Person #2 reads all the possible answers; Person #3 selects the worst answer or answers—the throw-away items—and [explains] why, to reduce the options to two. Person #4 selects the right answer and says why.

When the right answer comes out—and it almost always is the right answer . . . because they have had the power of the group—everybody applauds for the whole table. They tackled it together. They leave with good positive feelings, almost like it's been a game show, so they look forward to taking an individual test because they have associated the experience with the group.

[We] sit on the floor in a circle with the test and debrief it . . . most of the time in groups. Nobody gets bored, and everyone is completely attentive. . . If someone got it wrong, they now understand why they got it wrong. They say why they selected that answer. . . . If they say there are three toss-away questions and only one makes sense, [they] say why. So they are developing some test savvy.

Through her approach to practice tests, Mrs. Pérez simulates the actual individual test-taking method, knowing that her students must develop particular skills. But she incorporates a group process during the practice-test debriefing. As the group analyzes how to answer questions, students are helping each other gain metacognitive awareness about how to take tests.

The process used in Mrs. Pérez's classroom addresses several of the pitfalls students commonly face: inaccurate reading of the question, failure to critically choose one of two remaining potential answers (rather than just pick one), and failure to check one's answers (see Calkins, Montgomery, & Santman, 1999). Although students do not routinely paraphrase each question (a recommended strategy, according to Calkins and her colleagues), the meaning of the question is quite likely clarified as the students reread it and discuss rationales for various answers. Misunderstandings that remain are cleared up when students present to the class in their small groups. Although the debriefing method entails checking answers, it does not address the problem that students face when they have to check their answers on the actual test by themselves—something many students apparently find daunting. (See Calkins, Montgomery,

& Santman,1999, for some excellent suggestions for dealing with this issue.)

Test prep in Ms. Daley's class. Ms. Daley's reflections on standardized testing show how her own experience as a student influenced how she administered tests initially—and how she developed a more group-oriented approach later on:

> The only way that I could give the test was how I remember taking the test when I was in school. You couldn't talk or look at another person's paper. It was extremely individualistic. If you didn't understand the question, the teacher would say, "Do the best you can." We were on our own. Yet when I gave the test, every day I came out feeling absolutely awful, and the other teachers would say, "They will never do very well on the test. It's not a complete reflection on you; the kids naturally forget half of the stuff you teach them." I felt very frustrated by it. Every year at that time I was frustrated, and year after year, the tests became more and more important in student as well as teacher assessment.
>
> Bridging Cultures began at that time. We had just gotten the first set of practice-test booklets to prepare students for the standardized test. Both Bridging Cultures and the new test materials together put such a focus on testing for me . . . When it came time to prepare for the test, I had the materials I needed and the format. All I needed was a style or a process I would use. I thought that a lot of the classes I had taken on cooperative learning worked so well with Bridging Cultures. It would be easy to have groups for test preparation!
>
> We would put the question on the board or overhead and work on it as a group, or [we would] just work out of one booklet—but always in a group. I still do this. I prefer to work my class in small or whole groups. Little by little, we move away from the whole group, as we get ready for the actual test. I make sure to explain to the students what changes are going to occur regarding group and individual work.

Isaac (1999) documented an instance of test preparation in Ms. Daley's classroom. The children in her class were taking a Stanford-9 practice exam. The children were seated in groups and were reading the questions aloud at their own pace. At one table, four children were pointing to the test and discussing the correct answer. The teacher left the classroom and said, "If you need help, help each other." A boy in the class doesn't know where to read and says this aloud. A student, Derek, comes to this boy to show him where the class is on the practice exam. Another boy from across the room comes to show the same boy where the class is on the exam as well (Isaac, 1999, p. 39).

Test prep in a non-Bridging Cultures class. The incident does not seem especially remarkable until it is contrasted with a test practice session in another non–Bridging Cultures 2nd grade classroom, composed primarily of immigrant Latino students.

During a Stanford-9 practice session, Gloria tries to hide her answers on her worksheet from Brent by folding the top of her paper up. On that same worksheet, Gloria says, "I only need five more." Brent says, "I have one, two, three, four more." Lourdes says, "I am on the second page" (Isaac, 1999, p. 37). The competitive nature of behavior in the second classroom contrasts with the collaborative nature of behavior in Ms. Daley's classroom.

The power of the group. Ms. Daley observed that students not only achieved higher test scores, they did not feel dumb, and they perceived the testing as more fun. They understood the skill needed to be successful on the test. They had explored it in groups until they were able to do it alone. They stayed on task longer.

Both Mrs. Pérez and Ms. Daley used the power of the group to support students' success on standardized tests, whether in preparing them for the test or through debriefings on the answers to practice tests. Given the same cultural framework and professional development opportunities, these two teachers focused on different ends of the testing process—one on understanding the questions, the other on answers—but both used the students' cultural value orientation of helping as a tool for group preparation to support individual test performance.

ASSIGNING GRADES

Grades are sometimes touted as motivators to students. Grades may be equated with rewards or "pay" for work well done (see Brookhart, 2004; Hiner, 1973). But grades do not always function as motivators, particularly for low-performing students. Perhaps of most interest in the context of this book is the question of how Bridging Cultures teachers award grades when students are working collaboratively. Do they give individual grades? Do they give a group grade? Mr. Mercado explained how he grades students in groups:

> In terms of correcting collaborative work, I usually give all members the same number grade [based on a scale of 1 to 4]. The scoring rubric is always posted on the board alongside a specific criteria chart mandated by [the Los Angeles Unified School District] so there is no ambiguity. If the assignment involves writing, illustrating, presenting orally, etc., students will generally assign those tasks to those who they feel are best suited to do those specific jobs. You have to be very careful sometimes of who is asked to do what when you have special education students or new English language learners.
>
> Sometimes I may have to assign jobs to certain students at the beginning of the year, but later on everyone is chosen readily. Usually they work with the students found closest to them. Every Friday, my students have the option of changing their seats so no one sits in the same cluster for too long. Every so often you will get someone who prefers to work alone. If the assignment can be completed either way, I will allow this.

An example of an activity for which Mr. Mercado gives a group grade is the "found poem," created in 15 minutes by groups of five students. In this activity, students search through their literature books for a phrase that appeals to them. Then each member of the group writes a sentence in reaction to the phrase. As a group, the students agree on how to arrange their sentences in a certain order to create the "found poem." Reminding the students that they would get a group grade for their effort, Mr. Mercado asked a student, "What would a '4' look like on this?" The student replied, "Neat and getting along." Another student added, "Spelling and punctuation." When Mr. Mercado asked what might account for a "2," a student said, "Bad spelling."

In explaining how she grades group work on a project, Ms. Daley said she gives the group "an overall grade based on effort and product. I very rarely grade [students individually on] group projects. Normally, when they work in groups, they still have to complete the same kind of task individually as well. The investigation or exploration was the group work." So Ms. Daley has other opportunities to evaluate students' progress individually. However, she does not feel the need to determine individual grades for students engaged in group work.

When Mrs. Pérez's students work in groups, she sometimes gives individual grades as well as a group grade. She has used the individual/group grade approach with students ranging from 3rd graders to university graduate students. As she explained,

> Everybody contributes to the project and must be accountable. [Their work] must be visible and gradable. For example, if they are to make some kind of chart, map, or poster, they must divide the material fairly and demonstrate that they know it and can teach it. Each member of a cooperative group uses a different color marker to contribute his/her info on the project . . . A rubric is developed together, and the project—and each person's performance—is evaluated according to the agreed-upon rubric.

We can see that each of these three teachers has worked out ways to grade groups of students. Mrs. Pérez has the most elaborate system for ensuring individual as well as group accountability. All Bridging Cultures teachers address both individual and group performance. However, they have found different ways of doing so.

Group Grades as Motivators

Whether grades are actually motivators for students is a question we have not investigated in the Bridging Cultures Project. However, the issue of giving group or individual grades for group work deserves some thought. If students are group-oriented, then giving group grades for selected group work will likely be more motivating than giving individual grades. Group-oriented students may not be so interested in individual grades until they have been socialized to believe that those individual grades are important, based on their experiences in U.S. classrooms. Emphasizing grades has associated risks: the practice may unnecessarily put students in competition with each other, sometimes inadvertently prompting what would generally be recognized as cheating (presenting others' work as one's own); as students progress through school, they may come to focus on grades over learning—eliminating challenging courses or projects in order to maintain a desired grade-point average (see Trumbull, 2000).

In deciding which type of grades are motivating—individual or group—it would probably be best to ask the students from time to time if they would like to be evaluated for group work as individuals or as a group. This would allow the teacher to know explicitly what kind of grading seems more motivating. It would also be interesting for teachers to ask students the reason for their choice. In some cases, a hybrid evaluation might be appropriate. Students could get a certain percentage for the group grade and then explain in writing exactly what their contributions were to the group's product for the remaining percentage of the total grade. In our experience, this has worked successfully in higher education, though it has not, to our knowledge, been tried with younger students.

HELPING VERSUS CHEATING

Discussion of students helping each other prepare for standardized tests evokes questions about what counts as *helping* versus *cheating*. "A long-standing tradition in education holds that knowledge is valuable. . . Cheating can be seen as an attempt, by deceptive or fraudulent means, to represent oneself as possessing knowledge. In testing specifically, cheating is violating the rules" (Cizek, 1999, p. 3). Usual characterizations of cheating entail copying another's work, communicating an answer to another student, obtaining unauthorized information about a test, or taking unauthorized information into a testing situation. Copying material from a book and failing to acknowledge the source (i.e., plagiarizing) is also typically considered cheating (Cizek, 1999).

Learning all of the rules about what counts as cheating in U.S. classrooms is a developmental process, something no doubt more difficult for students from "nonmainstream" cultures. In the meantime, moral judgments may often be made about students who try to help others based on the values they learned at home. Words such as *lying, dishonesty, misrepresenting, deception,* and *morality* appear in the literature on cheating and may be applied to situations in which students are engaged in behaviors they do not realize are "wrong" in school terms (Athanasou & Olasehinde, 2002). The line between helping (an ethical behavior) and cheating (an unethical behavior) is culturally inscribed and variable. Where the line is drawn is related to cultural differences in conceptions of the purposes of schooling, notions of how knowledge is constructed, the nature and meaning of assessment, and the relationship between the individual and the group (Fleck, 2000; Greenfield, 1994; Nelson-LeGall & Resnick, 1998). Bridging Cultures teachers are likely to answer questions about what constitutes helping versus cheating differently from their non–Bridging Cultures colleagues. In an interview, Ms. Daley discussed cheating and how the children behaved when she "wasn't looking":

> When I first started teaching at [this school], there was, "No cheating. Nobody can help. You are doing your own work, so I know what you are capable of doing." [As it was,] nobody appeared capable of doing anything. So, it seemed to me that [this was] because I didn't even let them use [the skills that] make them the best learners: each other. So I got rid of the whole idea of cheating except when I introduce the tests. But aside from that, when we're learning how to take the test, I encourage them to "Help each other please, help each other out." (Isaac, 1999, p. 39)

Ms. Daley makes the rules about helping explicit (including when helping is *not* allowed); hence the question of what is cheating is not left to students' imagination or chance. As a result, misinterpretation of behaviors and unfair punishments are avoided. And although Mrs. Pérez does not talk about cheating per se, like Ms. Daley, she heads off possible misunderstandings by making very clear what kinds of helping are permitted in various contexts.

Whereas teachers may believe that it is perfectly clear what constitutes cheating in their classrooms, in reality there is considerable ambiguity, and the same behaviors may mean different things at different times. Some researchers have addressed the fact that the difference between helping and cheating is not absolute but has to do with the context in which behaviors are happening:

> In cooperative learning, where students work together to achieve common goals, knowledge is the property of the group; no misrepresentation or deprivation has taken place. Further, no rules are violated; in fact, quite the opposite. In cooperative learning contexts, the rules explicitly encourage collaboration and sharing information. (Cizek, 1999, p. 3)

According to Cizek, a teacher who fails to enforce distinctions between these two sets of expectations (demonstrating individual knowledge versus cooperating to produce shared knowledge) is exhibiting behavior that is "reprehensible and antithetical to the ethical values all teachers should knowingly or unknowingly inculcate" (1999, p. 5). But teachers' ideas about the role of helping in cooperative learning situations may differ from those of many of their students.

The Importance of Being Explicit About Helping Versus Cheating

Examples in the literature on cheating suggest that teachers generally make tacit assumptions about what counts as cheating and expect their students to know those assumptions (see Cizek, 1999; Fleck, 2000). What happens when a teacher interprets a student's helping behavior as "cheating"? First, the interpretation excludes important opportunities for a student to use his or her culture-based strengths and reduces potential learning opportunities for the student being helped—and for the student doing the helping. Second, it may also cause internal conflict for a student who has been brought up to be unselfish and help others, whereas the teacher is admonishing the student for that same behavior in school. Third, if behaviors are mistakenly labeled "cheating," the accusation can create long-lasting resentment or feelings of injustice that influence students' classroom participation and educational choices in the future.

We should point out that it is not only immigrant students whose norms about helping vary from those of the mainstream. Research suggests that American Indian and Alaska native students from intact communities tend to have a highly collaborative approach to learning and expectations that differ from those of dominant-culture students about when helping is appropriate (Edgewater, 1981; McAlpine & Taylor, 1993; Nelson-Barber & Dull, 1998). Some research has shown that African American students are more likely to want to help each other in the classroom and quite likely do not understand why such behavior is often prohibited (Gillies, 1999; Nelson-LeGall & Resnick, 1998). So the cross-cultural conflict around helping versus cheating may be more widespread than generally believed.

Benefits of Using the Power of the Group

We believe that using the power of the group, particularly among students from collectivistic cultures, makes great sense in preparing students for assessment. When possible, it would undoubtedly be beneficial to students to participate in debriefing discussions about actual assessments in the ways discussed in this chapter. In addition, occasional teacher interviews of students, probing why students responded as they did to test questions they may have found difficult, can reveal how cultural differences influence students' cognition (Solano-Flores, Trumbull, & Nelson-Barber, 2002). Substantial research supports the belief that allowing students to help each other learn is a good thing (see, for example, O'Donnell, 2006; Palincsar & Brown, 1984; Webb, 1991). Those who receive information perform better, and those who give it may clarify their own understanding (Gillies, 1999; O'Donnell, 2006). But students may not offer or ask for help from each other when they perceive that classroom expectations run to the contrary. In such cases, important cognitive resources are closed to students. Attitudes toward helping are somewhat schizophrenic: helping is often embraced as a source of student success, but the manner of providing it and the degree to which it is permitted are commonly constrained in order to conform to expectations of the dominant culture. Hence students may be getting mixed messages, and those from nondominant cultures may have more trouble sorting them out than their dominant-culture peers.

Bridging Cultures teachers know that their students' home culture values helping. The teachers' applications of that knowledge to assessment practices are important not only because they are culturally compatible for many students but also because they are sound practices that support learning and the ability to show what one has learned. As we observed earlier, these teachers are creating with their students a hybrid culture in the classroom that is constituted of home-culture practices and values as well as "mainstream" schooling practices and values (Gutiérrez, Baquedano-Lopez, & Tejeda, 1999). It could be argued that after a few years in the U.S. educational system, students adapt to school-culture norms, including rules about helping and cheating. This is quite likely true to some degree but is not always the case. On the other hand, increasing harmony between home and school may result in improved student performance and prevent immigrant and other students from opting out of the educational system (see Lipka, 1998; Nieto, 1999; Tharp, Estrada, Dalton, & Yamauchi, 2000).

◆ ◆ ◆ ◆ ◆

Given the diversity of values represented in classrooms, it is clear that rules about helping and cheating must be established and made explicit to everyone in the school community: to teachers, to students, and to families. Unfortunately, because it is assumed that everybody knows what it is, most treatments of cheating begin at the level of how to eliminate it rather than coming to a consensus on a definition.

Research on cheating is not as helpful as one might hope. The preponderance of it is concerned with college-age students, and when it addresses culture, it usually focuses on how to teach foreign students U.S. norms. Many college and university Web sites list campus policies on cheating. On occasion, they address "problems" with foreign students and cheating. With the exception of a few researchers, the education community does not seem to realize that the same cultural variability is an issue in the K–12 arena. Hayner and Bartzis (2005) note that universities need to understand that "cheating" is not a universally agreed-upon concept. Students from countries that value sharing and collaboration encounter difficulties when they come to the United States to study. They note that "academic honesty" must be considered as a cultural construct (p. 4) and that educators can do better by students when they understand common areas of conflict such as when helping is allowed and when it is not. For instance, in countries as diverse as Burma, Costa Rica, and Russia, learning is seen as a group task, and emphasis is placed on supporting the success of the group.

Without an understanding of cultural variation in what is considered cheating, teachers risk attributing incorrect motives to many immigrant students as well as other nonmainstream students whose implicit definitions of learning include helping each other. Cultural understanding should be brought to bear in the earliest stages of a student's education, before the student is implicitly labeled "morally deviant" by a teacher. In fact, students are sometimes referred for counseling or evaluation on the basis of behavior that is judged deviant rather than recognized as simply different from behavior accepted by the dominant culture (Hoover & Collier, 1985).

The examples in this chapter suggest possible ways teachers might make assessment practices culturally harmonious, but more research in this area is clearly needed. Research on various approaches to organizing test preparation and practice with students from different backgrounds could contribute to our understanding of what works for whom. It would be interesting to study the practice of group test preparation versus individual test preparation systematically, with different populations of students, to determine if there are differences in test outcomes.

CONCLUSION

[T]he ultimate goal of classroom management is not to achieve compliance or control, but to provide all students with equitable opportunities for learning.

—Carol Weinstein, Mary Curran, and Saundra Tomlinson-Clarke, "Culturally Responsive Classroom Management: Awareness into Action," in *Theory into Practice*

An analysis of 50 years of research concluded that "*classroom management is the single greatest influence on student learning*—greater than students' cognitive processes (such as general intelligence, prior knowledge), home environment, motivation, and socioeconomic status" (Weinstein & Mignano, 2003, p. 6, citing Wang, Haertel, & Wahlberg, 1993–1994). What are we to make of this finding? Our first reaction is likely to be shock and disbelief. Yet upon reflection, it is not so amazing. After all, positive management practices, or what we call "classroom orchestration," are necessary for classroom harmony and productivity—essential conditions for student success. Because classroom management practices establish and maintain the quality and efficiency of the learning environment, they can either support or impede learning at every level.

WHERE HAVE WE BEEN AND WHERE ARE WE GOING?

One of the most notable changes in recent years is the move away from behavioristic approaches to classroom organization and management toward approaches that are more in line with developmental and constructivist perspectives (see, for example, Carter & Doyle, 2006;

Elias & Schwab, 2006; Freiberg & Lapointe, 2006; Kohn, 1996; Nucci, 2006; Watson & Battistich, 2006).[1] Many of these new ways of thinking about classroom management cast it as a "social and moral curriculum" (Evertson & Weinstein, 2006, p. 12), in which relationships between teachers and students are key. For example, Freiberg (1999) offers a person-centered classroom management model that includes a focus on "caring, guidance, cooperation, and the building of self-discipline" (p. 13). Freiberg and Lapointe (2006) cite evidence that classroom management models are moving in the direction of recognizing the importance of "creating an environment of shared responsibility and learning" (p. 773).

An emphasis on students' self-discipline and self-regulation of learning reflects a developmental outlook. From this point of view, the teacher's role is not to control but to facilitate students' increasing ability to take responsibility for their actions as they mature. Another example of the shift away from behaviorism is called "developmental discipline," a "child-centered approach to classroom management that views children as active, willing partners in their own socialization, and is oriented toward the development of self-control and the internalization of prosocial values" (Battistich, Watson, Solomon, Schaps, & Solomon, 1991, p. 12).

Although we applaud the shift in thinking about classroom management toward developmental and constructivist perspectives, we lament the fact that most of the theory, research, and literature about classroom organization and management continue to largely ignore the role of culture. This lack of attention is probably not a result of disregard for the importance of culture, but a consequence of being overwhelmed by the nuances of so many cultures coming together in many classrooms in the United States. Knowing about all the cultural backgrounds of students even in one class can be daunting, as expressed so well by Mrs. Eyler in Chapter 1 and worth repeating

---

[1] Behavioral techniques for managing behavior may be necessary for students with developmental problems in special education settings or in inclusive classrooms (Lane, Falk, & Wehby, 2006). There are ethical and effective ways for shaping desired social behaviors of such students (Landrum & Kauffman, 2006). However, a generalized behavioristic approach to organization and management is not consonant with current understandings of how children learn best.

here: "The children in my class came from so many distinct regions of Mexico and Central and South America, each with differing histories and traditions. I knew that I would never know enough. I had to give up trying." The task of understanding many cultures can seem almost impossible to teachers. We hope it is evident to readers that, although it is challenging, learning about students' cultures is worth the effort, and such learning can be greatly facilitated by frameworks (such as the individualism/collectivism framework presented in this book) that help to explain clusters of characteristics of many cultures.

CULTURE AND THE INSIDERS' PERSPECTIVES

Fries and Cochran-Smith (2006) suggest that until we have "rich insiders' perspectives on the daily work of managing to teach, we will not have an adequate understanding of how teachers negotiate the complexities of the classroom" (p. 947). In this regard, we have been very fortunate to have the insiders' perspectives of our Bridging Cultures teachers. As a team, we have been able to consider the teachers in action and have them describe, explain, and reflect on their classroom orchestration immediately after an observation. We have also had the luxury of meeting with the teachers over a five-year period and conducting in-depth interviews to see which practices have endured, which have been modified, which have been jettisoned altogether and—above all—why these modifications have occurred.

The *why* of the teachers' changed classroom practices is perhaps the most significant contribution of the Bridging Cultures Project. "Among the most important beliefs teachers have about students are beliefs about the causes of their behavior and misbehavior" (Fries & Cochran-Smith, 2006, p. 959). If teachers have only one lens through which to see student behavior (in this case, the individualistic one espoused by schools), they are likely to unconsciously perceive helping as cheating or looking down as a sign of guilt rather than respectfulness. This is why an understanding of differing belief or value systems can be so generative for educators as they try to understand

and plan for classroom management and why a two-part framework as an organizing starting point can be highly valuable in efforts to improve classroom orchestration.

As we have seen in Bridging Cultures classrooms, teachers' practices can promote students' sense of belonging and competence when they actively draw upon students' culture-based strengths. McCarthy and Benally's (2003) study of classroom management in a Navajo middle school, one of the few actual studies that address the relations between classroom management and culture, reached similar conclusions. In fact, many of the same strategies Bridging Cultures teachers used were also successful with Navajo students, whose culture is highly collectivistic.

PROCEEDING CAUTIOUSLY IN THE CULTURAL DOMAIN— BUT PROCEEDING NONETHELESS

We caution readers to bear in mind that the approach we present in this book has limitations. First, the cultural individualism/collectivism framework is a heuristic, or tool, for cultural exploration. As they say, "The map is not the territory," and neither is the framework a full representation of the values of any one person or group of people. Second, cultures are not fully distinct, fixed entities. Cultures overlap in their values; they simply vary in the degree of emphasis placed on different values. Third, the "cultural patterns" of human existence we examine constitute only one piece of a complex tapestry that includes people's economic situation, their personal and group histories over generations, their home language and its status in the larger society, and the power relations between the group they identify with and the dominant cultural group in the society.

However, if we give up trying to understand culture, we have lost a powerful source of knowledge about how children learn and how classrooms can be orchestrated. Understanding how the collectivistic values that are espoused at home are often in conflict with the individualistic values of schools is germane to more than teachers of immigrant Latino students. According to Triandis (1989), 70 percent of cultures fall on the collectivistic side of the individualistic and collectivistic spectrum. Families with African, Asian, Central and South American, American Indian, Alaska Native, and Pacific Islander roots are *all* likely to rear their children more toward a collectivistic orientation than an individualistic one (Greenfield, 1994; Lipka et. al., 1998; Nelson-Barber, Trumbull, & Wenn, 2000).

CURRENT THREATS TO CLASSROOM ORCHESTRATION

The national desperation to improve educational outcomes for students, particularly those from ethnic and linguistic minority groups, has led to some positive and some unfortunate moves by states and districts. It can be argued that the establishment of content-area standards (what students should know and be able to do in various subject areas) and performance standards (what counts as doing well in a content area) has been a good step toward quality control in education. Of course, in the absence of equitable opportunities to learn and equitable testing, holding students to uniform standards can be unfair (see Meier [2000] for a scathing critique of the standards movement). In addition, the high-stakes testing that has resulted from federal efforts to assess districts' and states' educational outcomes has driven some districts to make choices that have some distinctly negative and unwanted outcomes (see, for example, Abedi, 2004; McNeil, 2000).

In an effort to boost students' state test scores, some districts have turned to packaged curriculum and reform programs. For example, the Los Angeles Unified School District (LAUSD), where most of the Bridging Cultures teachers teach, adopted the highly scripted Open Court reading program during the 2000–2001 school year. This program, which is only marginally adapted for English language learners (who constitute a large percentage of students in LAUSD), virtually forecloses teacher creativity in the organization of lessons or units (Girard, 2003; Trumbull, Rothstein-Fisch, & Hernandez, 2003). It also shuts parents out of the classroom—at least during the hours devoted to the program—because there is no way they can participate.

Many LAUSD teachers decry the near robotic behaviors associated with Open Court and the lack of opportunity to use their professional knowledge in instruction (Girard, 2003). Shortly after mandating Open Court, the district layered on the latest version of Lee and Marlene Canter's Assertive Discipline program. As a result, not only teachers' judgments about how to organize a key area of instruction but also their judgments about how to manage their classrooms were being challenged. These programs reflect a move back toward behavioristic methods and away from developmental, constructivist, and sociocultural approaches to teaching and learning.

Challenging the old, standard approaches to classroom organization and management is no small feat. Behavioristic notions, particularly the belief that children need to be controlled, are pervasive and tenacious in the teaching profession. During an assessment project meeting in New York City that Elise attended, teachers were lamenting the classroom management challenges of having a substitute teacher in their classes. The context was an informal discussion, and the teachers agreed that establishing who is boss and instilling in students an awareness of consequences for misbehavior were keys to being a successful teacher. "I really laid down the law and got them straightened out," said one 5th grade teacher of his students. We would venture to say that this is standard wisdom.

Clearly, our Bridging Cultures teachers are the authority in their classrooms, but the threat of punishment is not imminent. Somehow, these teachers have managed not only to command enormous respect but also to bring out the best in their students by going with the cultural flow, or "work[ing] with, rather than against, student nature" (Charles, 2000, p. 8, cited in Gay, 2006, p. 345).

WHAT CAN TEACHERS DO?

There is nothing quite so educationally powerful as an informed teacher, and this is particularly true when it comes to promoting good classroom practice. It is our experience, within the Bridging Cultures Project as well as other teacher research projects we have participated in, that when teachers have the opportunity to make their own knowledge explicit in the company of other professionals *and* to expand that knowledge, they find themselves empowered to carry out meaningful innovations in their classrooms and schools. So our answer to the question "What can teachers do?" is "A great deal." The Bridging Cultures teachers who teach in the Los Angeles Unified School District have found ways to adapt the Open Court activities and make time for the collaborative instruction they know works best for their students. Because they do not have discipline problems in their classes, they may regard the Assertive Discipline approach as unnecessary and avoid it without consequences.

By working closely with families, teachers can help put district mandates in perspective and collaborate to devise strategies for collectively addressing students' best interests. When teachers feel confident in using their professional knowledge, they can interpret policies intelligently for themselves, colleagues, and parents; working together they can marshal the resources to challenge ill-advised policies. We have seen this phenomenon among the Bridging Cultures teachers when school rules conflict with cultural values of students' families. Recall the example from Chapter 3, in which Mr. Mercado realized that parents whose children were bused to school faced difficulties in getting transportation to come to the school for parent conferences. Rather than ignore the problem, he went to the children's home neighborhoods to conduct the conferences there; the school eventually provided a bus to enable the parents to come to the school. Another example comes from bilingual educators who have identified assessment policies that unfairly penalize their students and succeeded in changing them (Trumbull & Koelsch, in press).

EXPANDING ON WHAT WE KNOW: FUTURE RESEARCH QUESTIONS

Future research can add to what we know about cultural values and classroom management and explore effective ways to expand the use of successful practices. Here we suggest a few research questions to begin the process.

What would be the effects—if any—of incorporating Bridging Cultures into preservice teacher education programs? It is one thing to collaborate intensively with seven experienced and talented teachers and follow their processes of change closely over a period of several years. It is another to reach significant numbers of teachers and teachers-in-training. Quite naturally, we wonder whether incorporating Bridging Cultures as an integrated body of content in courses and field-based experiences would help teachers begin their careers with a cultural perspective that would permeate their thinking and practice. Would such teachers examine accepted practice related to organization and management with a view to tailoring it to tap the culture-based strengths of their students? If new teachers working in Latino and other collectivistic communities knew where to begin in exploring the values and expectations of families, would they be able to reduce disharmony and the amount of time wasted in trying to shape behaviors that do not come naturally and, perhaps, are not even necessary?

This question has not been asked in terms of classroom management, but the appeal and apparent utility of the Bridging Cultures approach and classroom examples to prospective teachers has been demonstrated. Education students at California State University, Northridge, have had a very positive response to the individualism/collectivism framework. Graduate students have examined the framework as it relates to parent-teacher conferences (Hernandez, 2003) and parent-involvement workshops (Beckley, 2002; Chaparro, 2001; Garfio, 2002; Guzman & Martinez, 2002) and in terms of innovations for school counselors (Geary, 2000; Roman, 2006). In this book we have demonstrated how understanding culture affected classroom orchestration (though that was not an expressed intent of the project) as well as organization of subject matter content areas and assessment. Bridging Cultures as a theoretical model of development, based on research and field-tested by teachers, can permeate many kinds of teacher education courses, not just those dedicated to classroom management. For example, courses in educational psychology, methods courses in the content areas, or courses on assessment might also make use of the framework for organizing thinking about student learning. Through multiple exposures to the notions of individualism and collectivism, students could explore the impact of culture on education in a fashion somewhat like our Bridging Cultures teachers—that is, over time.

What effects might Bridging Cultures have in culturally heterogeneous classrooms or in monocultural classrooms with dominant-culture students? Different kinds of student populations suggest another set of research questions. What might teachers trained in Bridging Cultures concepts do in heterogeneous classrooms, where students come from diverse cultural backgrounds—some very collectivistic and others very individualistic? How would teachers make choices about organization and management? What might the results be, socially and academically? How would cultural knowledge be useful to teachers in monocultural classrooms of dominant-culture students? We speculate that understanding the role of culture in classroom organization and management (and in education in general) would prepare teachers to be more flexible and context-sensitive in their strategies and relationships with students and families—no matter what the cultural constitution of their classrooms in this multicultural society.

How can families be supported to come to the forefront? An equally important arena for research on the usefulness of the Bridging Cultures approach is the family-community realm. In relation to organization and management, researchers might convene groups of parents and family members to discuss classroom organization and management topics, using the individualism/collectivism framework as a way to organize discussion topics and questions. Teachers themselves could carry out such activities in the form of action research. If families were approached as equals in a process of exploration, their voices might be heard and heeded more than is often the case, and valuable data could be added to the literature on classroom organization and management. "[O]ne way to move the parent-school dialogue forward in a meaningful manner for all involved is to allow parents' life experiences and cultural capital to inform schools' cultural worlds" (Carreón, Drake, & Barton, 2005, p. 494). If the goal is to have a classroom in which a hybrid culture develops, built on home and school cultural models, then families must be included in this way.

THE BEST OF BOTH WORLDS: OPERATING WITH KNOWLEDGE, UNDERSTANDING, AND FLEXIBILITY

Although the majority of our examples have indicated a shift from conventional individualistic approaches to more collectivistic approaches to classroom organization, the idea that *both* kinds of practices are needed is worth repeating. With their knowledge of individualism and collectivism, Bridging Cultures teachers came to understand themselves, their students and their families, and their schools much better. Their new knowledge provided them with the flexibility to reconceptualize and reorganize their classrooms in innovative ways that promoted student learning. The teachers never adopted a set of strategies suggested by researchers; they simply noticed areas for potential change and modified their classrooms accordingly. The choice between a collectivistic and an individualistic classroom is not an either/or decision, but rather a both/and decision, with the caveat that classroom rules, procedures, and activities need to be explicit as to their intention. Making intentions explicit might include a demonstration or discussion of getting help with achievement (such as the buddy system and the star chart mentioned in Chapter 7) or, as in the case of standardized testing, an explanation of when and how to work alone.

With regard to the implementation of collectivistic strategies with students from more individualistic cultures, we would argue that creating a "village," as Mr. Mercado calls it, would be beneficial to those students as well. The proliferation of literature on classrooms as learning communities attests to the recognition that a group orientation has advantages. In their inspiring and thought-provoking book *The Good Society* (1991), Robert Bellah and his coauthors say this:

> It should be obvious that learning is never the result of the efforts of isolated, competitive individuals alone, and that the evident weakness in American schools has much to do with the weakening of their community context. The weakening of community and the erosion of the cultural endowment upon which a viable community is based go hand and hand. (p. 172)

Teachers who have learned about the individualism/collectivism framework and its potential application to classroom organization and management are likely to be in a far better position to nurture learning communities, where the "cooperative and interactional nature of learning" (Bellah et al., 1991, p. 172) is emphasized. We would like to see research that explores whether that is the case.

Another aspect of knowledge, understanding, and flexibility is how teachers came to know what kinds of classroom strategies were most needed by their particular students. To illustrate this point, we contrast two Bridging Cultures teachers. One teacher, working with the most rural families, produced the most collectivistic classroom. On the other hand, one teacher moved to a more middle-class neighborhood during the project, and her collectivistic strategies for engaging parent volunteers did not work nearly as well as they had in her previous school. The lesson learned is that strategies must be adapted for the context.

FINAL THOUGHTS

In 1971, Seymour Sarason wrote an influential book on school reform titled *The Culture of the School and the Problem of Change*. In it, Sarason argued that reforms that focus on curriculum, instruction, or school organization without regard for the culture of the school cannot be expected to succeed. Sarason's premise was that "the school's culture, the very fabric of its existence is what must be changed" (Gallimore & Goldenberg, 2001, p. 46). We are, in essence, arguing for the same thing more than 35 years later—for awareness of school culture and how it does or does not support student access to equitable education. Echoing Weinstein and colleagues (2003), we urge our readers to remember that the main goal of classroom organization and management is "to provide all students with equitable opportunities for learning" (p. 275).

Classroom management and organization are a function not only of teachers' values, beliefs, and expectations, but also of their knowledge about possibilities. A single cultural point of view can blind teachers to the potential right before their eyes. If teachers do not even see the different skills that students have, but only gaps in the expected skills, they will waste or damage precious human resources. This is why learning about culture—one's own culture, the culture of school, and the culture of home—is essential.

Some have expressed concern about the risks of oversimplifying the concept of "culture" and of misapplying generalizations about different cultural groups (see Gutiérrez & Rogoff, 2003), with regrettable outcomes. However, such concern should not prevent us from making the effort to learn about culture. Cultural differences do exist and are relevant. "The concept of culture provides us with the only way we know to speak about the differences between peoples of the world, differences that persist" (Kuper, 1999 cited in Paradise, 2002, p. 238). The greater risk is, thus, ignoring culture. As we have said before, to ignore culture is to hobble schooling.

REFERENCES

Abedi, J. (2004). The No Child Left Behind Act and English language learners: Assessment and accountability issues. *Educational Researcher, 33*(1), 1–14.

Abedi, J., Courtney, M., Mirocha, J., & Leon, S. (2005). Language accommodations for English language learners in large-scale assessments: Bilingual dictionaries and linguistic modification, CSE Report 666. Los Angeles: National Center for Research on Evaluation, Standards, and Student Testing (CRESST). Graduate School of Education and Information Studies (GSEIS), University of California.

Abedi, J., Leon, S., & Mirocha, J. (2001, April). *Validity of standardized achievement: Tests for English language learners.* Paper presented at the Annual Meeting of the American Educational Research Association. Seattle, WA.

Antil, L. R., Jenkins, J. R., & Wayne, S. K. (1998). Cooperative learning: Prevalence, conceptualizations, and the relation between research and practice. *American Educational Research Journal, 35*(3), 419–454.

Antrop-González, R., Vélez, W., & Garrett, T. (2003). Where are the academically successful Puerto Rican students? Five success factors of high achieving Puerto Rican high school students. JSRI Working Paper #61. East Lansing, MI: Julian Samora Research Institute, Michigan State University. Retrieved September 9, 2006, from http://www.jsri.msu.edu/RandS/research/wps/wp61.html

Athanasou, J. A., & Olasehinde, O. (2002). Male and female differences in self-report cheating. *Practical Assessment, Research & Evaluation, 8*(5). Retrieved June 2, 2007, from http://PAREonline.net/getvn.asp?v=8&n=5

Atwell, N. (1987). *In the middle: Writing, reading, and learning with adolescents.* Portsmouth, NH: Heinemann.

Au, K., & Jordan, C. (1981). Teaching reading to Hawaiian children: Analysis of a culturally appropriate instructional event. *Anthropology and Education Quarterly, 11,* 91–115.

August, D., & Hakuta, K. (1997). *Improving schooling for language-minority children.* Washington, DC: National Academy Press.

Battistich, V., Watson, M., Solomon, D., Schaps, E., & Solomon, J. (1991). The child development project: A comprehensive program for the development of prosocial character. In W. M. Kurtines & J. L. Gerwitz (Eds.), *Handbook of moral behavior and development* (Vol. 3, pp. 1–33). Hillsdale, NJ: Lawrence Erlbaum Associates.

Beaumont, C., de Valenzuela, J., & Trumbull, E. (2002). Alternative assessment for transitional readers. *Bilingual Research Journal, 26*(2), 241–268.

Beckley, L. (2002). *Bridging cultures between home and school literacy: Spanish speaking first graders and their families.* Unpublished master's thesis, California State University, Northridge.

Bellah, R., Madsen, R., Sullivan, W. M., Swidler, A., & Tipton, S. M. (1991). *The good society.* New York: Alfred A. Knopf.

Benard, B. (2004). *Resiliency: What we have learned.* San Francisco: WestEd.

Ben-Peretz, M., Eilam, B., & Yankelevitch, E. (2006). Classroom management in multicultural classes in an immigrant country: The case of Israel. In C. M. Evertson & C. S. Weinstein (Eds.), *Handbook of classroom management: Research, practice, and contemporary issues* (pp. 1121–1139). Mahwah, NJ: Lawrence Erlbaum Associates.

Betts, G. (2004). Fostering autonomous learners through levels of differentiation. *Roeper Review, 26*(4). Retrieved August 16, 2006, from http://www.apa.org/ed/tblofcontents53.html

Bowers, C. A., & Flinders, D. J. (1990). *Responsive teaching: An ecological approach to classroom patterns of language, culture, and thought.* New York: Teachers College Press.

Boykin, A. W., & Bailey, C. T. (2000). The role of cultural factors in school relevant cognitive functioning (Report No. 43). Baltimore: Center for Research on the Education of Students Placed at Risk [CRESPAR]. Retrieved April 4, 2005, from http://www.csos.jhu.edu/crespar/techReports/Report43.pdf

Bransford, J. D., Brown, A. L., & Cocking, R. R. (Eds.). (2000). *How people learn: Brain, mind, experience and school.* Washington, DC: National Academy Press.

Bredekamp, S., & Copple, C. (Eds.). (1997). *Developmentally appropriate practice in early childhood education* (Rev. ed.). Washington, DC: National Association for the Education of Young Children.

Brookhart, S. M. (2004). *Grading.* Upper Saddle River, NJ: Pearson/Merrill Prentice Hall.

Bruner, J. S. (1996). *The culture of education.* Cambridge, MA: Harvard University Press.

Cabello, B., & Burstein, N. (1995). Examining teachers' beliefs about teaching in culturally diverse classrooms. *Journal of Teacher Education, 46*(4), 285–294.

Calkins, L. M. (1983). *Lessons from a child: On the teaching and learning of writing.* Portsmouth, NH: Heinemann.

Calkins, L., Montgomery, K., & Santman, D. (1999). Helping children master the tricks and avoid the traps of standardized tests. *Practical Assessment, Research & Evaluation, 6*(8). Retrieved June 28, 2007, from http://PAREonline.net/getvn.asp?v=6&n=8

Canter, L., & Canter, M. (1992). *Lee Canter's assertive discipline: Positive behavior management for today's classroom* (Rev. ed.). Santa Monica, CA: Lee Canter & Associates.

Carlson, F. M. (2006). *Essential touch: Meeting the needs of young children.* Washington, DC: National Association for the Education of Young Children.

Carreón, G. P., Drake, C., & Barton, A. C. (2005). The importance of presence: Immigrant parents' school engagement experiences. *American Educational Research Journal, 42*(3), 465–498.

Carter, K., & Doyle, W. (2006). Classroom management in early childhood and elementary classrooms. In C. M. Evertson & C. S. Weinstein (Eds.), *Handbook of classroom management: Research, practice, and contemporary issues* (pp. 373–406). Mahwah, NJ: Lawrence Erlbaum Associates.

Caspe, M. S. (2003). How teachers come to understand families. *School Community Journal, 13*(1), 115–131.

Cazden, C. (2001). *Classroom discourse: The language of teaching and learning* (2nd ed.). Portsmouth, NH: Heinemann.

Centre for Promoting Learner Autonomy. (2006, February). *Promoting learner autonomy through assessment* [Briefing paper]. Retrieved August 16, 2006, from http://www.shu.ac.uk/cetl/autonomy/projectbriefs/christines.pdf

Chaparro, P. (2001). *Empowering parents of kindergarten students with strategies and skills for understanding school: Focus on reading readiness.* Unpublished master's thesis, California State University, Northridge.

Chen, X. (2006). *Struggling readers at the middle level: A cross-cultural study of the social aspect of their reading.* Unpublished dissertation, Texas Tech University, Lubbock.

Cizek, G. J. (1999). *Cheating on tests: How to do it, detect it and prevent it.* Mahwah, NJ: Lawrence Erlbaum Associates.

Cohen, E. (1994). Restructuring the classroom: Conditions for productive small groups. *Review of Educational Research, 64,* 1–35.

Cole, M., Engeström, Y., & Vasquez, O. (1997). *Mind, culture, and activity.* Cambridge, UK: Cambridge University Press.

Connors, L. J., & Epstein, J. L. (1995). Parent and school partnerships. In M. H. Bornstein (Ed.), *Handbook of parenting* (Vol. 4, *Applied and practical parenting,* pp. 437–458). Mahwah, NJ: Lawrence Erlbaum Associates.

Cooper, H. (2001, April). Homework for all—in moderation. *Educational Leadership, 58*(7), 34–38.

Daniels, H. (2002). *Literature circles: Voice and choice in the student-centered classroom.* York, ME: Stenhouse.

Deci, E. L., Koestner, R., & Ryan, R. M. (1999). A meta-analytic review of experiments examining the effects of extrinsic rewards on intrinsic motivation. *Psychological Bulletin, 125,* 627–668.

Deci, E. L., Koestner, R., & Ryan, R. M. (2001). Extrinsic rewards and intrinsic motivation in education: Reconsidered once again. *Review of Educational Research, 71*(1), 1–27.

Delgado-Gaitan, C. (1992). School matters in the Mexican-American home: Socializing children to education. *American Educational Research Journal, 29*(3), 495–513.

Delgado-Gaitan, C. (1994). Socializing young children in Mexican-American families: An intergenerational perspective. In P. M. Greenfield & R. R. Cocking (Eds.), *Cross-cultural roots of minority child development* (pp. 55–86). Hillsdale, NJ: Lawrence Erlbaum Associates.

Delgado-Gaitan, C. (1996). *Protean literacy: Extending the discourse on empowerment.* Washington, DC: Falmer Press.

Doyle, W. (2006). Ecological approaches to classroom management. In C. M. Evertson & C. S. Weinstein (Eds.), *Handbook of classroom management: Research, practice, and contemporary issues* (pp. 97–125). Mahwah, NJ: Lawrence Erlbaum Associates.

Durán, R. P. (1985). Influences of language skills on bilinguals' problem solving. In S. F. Chipman, J.W. Segal, & R. Glaser (Eds.), *Thinking and learning skills* (pp. 187–207). Hillsdale, NJ: Lawrence Erlbaum Associates.

Edgewater, L. I. (1981). Stress and the Navajo university student. *Journal of American Indian Education, 20* (3), 25–31.

Edwards, C. H. (2004). *Classroom discipline and management* (4th ed.). New York: Wiley.

Elias, M. J., & Schwab, Y. (2006). From compliance to responsibility: Social and emotional learning and classroom management. In C. M. Evertson, & C. S. Weinstein (Eds.), *Handbook of classroom management: Research, practice, and contemporary issues* (pp. 309–341). Mahwah, NJ: Lawrence Erlbaum Associates.

Ercikan, K. (2006). Developments in assessment of student learning. In P. A. Alexander & P. H. Winne (Eds.), *Handbook of educational psychology* (2nd ed., pp. 929–952). Mahwah, NJ: Lawrence Erlbaum Associates.

Evertson, C. M., Emmer, E. T., & Worsham, M. E. (2006). *Classroom management for elementary teachers* (7th ed). Boston: Allyn & Bacon.

Evertson, C. M., & Randolph, C. H. (1995). Classroom management in the learning-centered classroom. In A. C. Ornstein (Ed.), *Teaching: Theory and practice.* Boston: Allyn & Bacon.

Evertson, C. M., & Weinstein, C. S. (2006). Classroom management as a field of inquiry. In C. M. Evertson & C. S. Weinstein (Eds.), *Handbook of classroom management: Research, practice, and contemporary issues* (pp. 3–15). Mahwah, NJ: Lawrence Erlbaum Associates.

Fall, R., Webb, N. M., & Chudowsky, N. (2000). Group discussion and large-scale language arts assessment: Effects on students' comprehension. *American Educational Research Journal, 37,* 911–941.

Fallona, C., & Richardson, V. (2006). Classroom management as a moral activity. In C. M. Evertson & C. S. Weinstein (Eds.), *Handbook of classroom management: Research, practice, and contemporary issues* (pp. 1041–1062). Mahwah, NJ: Lawrence Erlbaum Associates.

Farr, B., & Trumbull, E. (1997). *Assessment alternatives for diverse classrooms.* Norwood, MA: Christopher-Gordon.

Fetterman, D. M. (1989). *Ethnography step by step. Applied Social Research Methods series* Volume 17. Newbury Park, CA: Sage Publications.

Fleck, C. (2000). Understanding cheating in Nepal. *Electronic Magazine of Multicultural Education, 2* (1). Available http://www.eastern.edu/publications/emme/2000spring/fleck.html.

Fox, M., & Wilkinson, L. (1997). No longer travelers in a strange country. *Journal of Children's Literature, 23*(1), 6–15.

Freiberg, H. J., (Ed.). (1999). *Beyond behaviorism: Changing the classroom management paradigm.* Boston: Allyn & Bacon.

180   Managing Diverse Classrooms

Freiberg, H. J., & Lapointe, J. M. (2006). Research-based programs for preventing and solving discipline problems. In C. M. Evertson & C. S. Weinstein (Eds.), *Handbook of classroom management: Research, practice, and contemporary issues* (pp. 735–786). Mahwah, NJ: Lawrence Erlbaum Associates.

Freire, P. (1970). *Pedagogy of the oppressed.* New York: Seabury Press.

Fries, K., & Cochran-Smith, M. (2006). Teacher research and classroom management: What questions do teachers ask? In C. M. Evertson & C. S. Weinstein (Eds.), *Handbook of classroom management: Research, practice, and contemporary issues* (pp. 945–981). Mahwah, NJ: Lawrence Erlbaum Associates.

Gallimore, R., & Goldenberg, C. (2001). Analyzing cultural models and settings to connect minority achievement and school improvement research. *Educational Psychologist, 36*(1), 45–56.

Gambrell, L. B., Mazzoni, S. A., & Almasi, J. F. (2000). Promoting collaboration, social interaction, and engagement with text. In L. Baker, M. J. Dreher, & J. T. Guthrie (Eds.), *Engaging young readers: Promoting achievement and motivation* (pp. 119–139). New York: Guilford Press.

Garfio, M. (2002). *Using the Bridging Cultures framework to empower the parents of second grade Spanish readers.* Unpublished master's thesis, California State University, Northridge.

Gay, G. (2006). Connections between classroom management and culturally responsive teaching. In C. M. Evertson & C. S. Weinstein (Eds.), *Handbook of classroom management: Research, practice, and contemporary issues* (pp. 343–370). Mahwah, NJ: Lawrence Erlbaum Associates.

Geary, J. P. (2000). *Bridging Cultures through school counseling: Theoretical understanding and practical solutions.* Unpublished master's thesis, California State University, Northridge.

Gillies, R. M. (1999). Maintenance of cooperative and helping behaviors in reconstituted groups. *Journal of Educational Research, 92* (6), 357–370.

Girard, K., & Koch, S. J. (1996). *Conflict resolution in the schools: A manual for educators.* San Francisco: Jossey-Bass.

Girard, V. (2003, February 20). *Open Court reading 2002: A practitioner's perspective.* Presentation to the Program Council of WestEd, San Francisco.

Goldenberg, C., & Gallimore, R. (1995). Immigrant Latino parents' values and beliefs about their children's education: Continuities and discontinuities across cultures and generations. *Advances in Motivation and Achievement, 9,* 183–228.

Greenfield, P. M. (1994). Independence and interdependence as developmental scripts: Implications for theory, research, and practice. In P. M. Greenfield & R. R. Cocking (Eds.), *Cross-cultural roots of minority child development* (pp. 1–37). Mahwah, NJ: Lawrence Erlbaum Associates.

Greenfield, P. M., Keller, H., Fuligni, A., & Maynard, A. (2003). Cultural pathways through universal development. *Annual Review of Psychology, 54,* 461–490.

Greenfield, P. M., Quiroz, B., & Raeff, C. (2000, Spring). Cross-cultural conflict and harmony in the social construction of the child. In S. Harkness, C. Raeff, & C. M. Super (Eds.), *New directions for child and adolescent development,* 87. San Francisco: Jossey-Bass.

Greenfield, P. M., Raeff, C., & Quiroz, B. (1996). Cultural values in learning and education. In B. Williams (Ed.), *Closing the achievement gap: A vision for changing beliefs and practices* (pp. 37–55). Alexandria, VA: Association for Supervision and Curriculum Development.

Greenfield, P. M., Suzuki, L., & Rothstein-Fisch, C. (2006). Cultural pathways through human development. In K. A. Renninger & I. E. Sigel (Eds.), *Handbook of child psychology* (6th ed., Vol. 4: *Child psychology in practice,* pp. 655–699). New York: Wiley.

Gutiérrez, K. D. (1994). How talk, context, and script shape contexts for learning: A cross-case comparison of journal sharing. *Linguistics and Education, 5,* 335–365.

Gutiérrez, K., Baquedano-López, P., Alvarez, H., & Chiu, M. (1999). A cultural-historical approach to collaboration: Building a culture of collaboration through hybrid language practices. *Theory into Practice, 38*(2), 87–93.

Gutiérrez, K., Baquedano-López, P., & Tejeda C. (1999). Rethinking diversity: Hybridity and hybrid language practices in the third space. *Mind, Culture, and Activity, 6*(4), 286–303.

Gutiérrez, K., & Rogoff, B. (2003). Cultural ways of learning: Individual traits or repertoires of practice. *Educational Researcher. 32*(5), 19–25.

Guzman, B., & Martinez, V. (2002). *Empowering parents of migrant preschoolers using the Bridging Cultures Framework*. Unpublished master's thesis, California State University, Northridge.

Harry, B., Allen, N., & McLaughlin, M. (1995). Communication versus compliance: African-American parents' involvement in special education. *Exceptional Children, 61*(4), 364–377.

Hayner, A., & Bartzis, O. L. (2005, November 7). *"Cheating" or "sharing:" Academic ethics across cultures*. Paper presented at NAFSA Region VI Conference, Louisville, KY.

Heath, S. B. (1983). *Ways with words: Language, life, and work in communities and classrooms*. Cambridge, England: Cambridge University Press.

Henderson, A. T., & Mapp, K. L. (2002). *A new wave of evidence: The impact of school, family, and community connections on student achievement*. Austin, TX: Southwest Educational Development Laboratory, National Center for Family & Community Connections with Schools.

Hernandez, R. (2003). *Reaching across the cultural bridge to collectivistic families: Kindergarten connections*. Unpublished master's thesis, California State University, Northridge.

Hiner, R. (1973). The cultural function of grading. *Clearing House, 47*, (6), 356-61.

Hofstede, G. (1991). *Culture's consequences*. Thousand Oaks, CA: Sage Publications.

Hofstede, G. (2001). *Culture's consequences: Comparing values, behaviors, institutions and organizations across nations* (2nd ed.). Thousand Oaks, CA: Sage Publications.

Hollins, E. R. (1996). *Culture in school learning: Revealing the deep meaning*. Mahwah, NJ: Lawrence Erlbaum Associates.

Hoover, J. H., & Collier, C. (1985). Referring culturally different children: Sociocultural considerations. *Academic Therapy, 20* (4), 503–509.

Hoover-Dempsey, K. V., Bassler, O. T., & Burrow, R. (1995). Parents' reported involvement in students' homework: Strategies and practices. *The Elementary School Journal, 95*(5), 435–449.

Hoover-Dempsey, K. V., & Sandler, H. M. (1997). Why do parents become involved in their children's education? *Review of Educational Research, 67*(1), 3–42.

Isaac, A. R. (1999). *How teachers' cultural ideologies influence children's relations inside the classroom: The effects of a cultural awareness teacher training program in two classrooms*. Unpublished psychology honors thesis, University of California, Los Angeles.

Johns, K. M., & Espinoza, C. (1996). *Management strategies for culturally diverse classrooms*. Bloomington, IN: Phi Delta Kappa Educational Foundation.

Johnson, D. W., & Johnson, R. T. (1994). *Learning together and alone: Cooperative, competitive, and individualistic learning* (4th ed.). Boston: Allyn & Bacon.

Johnson, D. W., Johnson, R. T., & Holubec, E. J. (1994). *The new circles of learning*. Alexandria, VA: Association for Supervision and Curriculum Development.

Jones, V. F., & Jones, L. S. (2007). *Comprehensive classroom management: Creating communities of support and solving problems* (8th ed.). Boston: Allyn & Bacon.

Kim, U., & Choi, S. (1994). Individualism, collectivism, and child development: A Korean perspective. In P. M. Greenfield & R. R. Cocking (Eds.), *Cross-cultural roots of minority child development* (pp. 227–258). Hillsdale, NJ: Lawrence Erlbaum Associates.

Kohn, A. (1993). *Punished by rewards: The trouble with gold stars, incentive plans, A's, praise, and other bribes*. Boston: Houghton Mifflin.

Kohn, A. (1996). *Beyond discipline: From compliance to community*. Alexandria, VA: Association for Supervision and Curriculum Development.

Lambert, W. E., Hammers, J. F., & Frasure-Smith, N. (1979). *Child-rearing values: A cross-national study*. New York: Praeger.

Landrum, T. J., & Kauffman, J. M. (2006). Behavioral approaches to classroom management. In C. M. Evertson & C. S. Weinstein (Eds.) *Handbook of classroom management: Research, practice, and contemporary issues* (pp. 47–71). Mahwah, NJ: Lawrence Erlbaum Associates.

Lane, K., Falk, K., & Wehby, J. (2006). Classroom management in special education classrooms and resource rooms. In C. M. Evertson & C. S. Weinstein (Eds.) *Handbook of classroom management: Research, practice, and contemporary issues* (pp. 439–460). Mahwah, NJ: Lawrence Erlbaum Associates.

Lee, A. R. (2005). *Character education: Helping our children to develop good character.* North Carolina Family Policy Council. Retrieved August 23, 2005, from www.ncfamily.org/PolicyPapers/Findings%200203-CharacterEd.pdf.

Levin, J., & Nolan, J. F. (2007). *Principles of classroom management: A professional decision-making model* (5th ed.). Boston: Allyn & Bacon.

Lewis, C. C. (1995). *Educating hearts and minds: Reflections on Japanese preschool and elementary education.* New York: Cambridge University Press.

Lewis, T. J., Newcomer, L. L., Trussell, R., & Richter, M. (2006). Schoolwide positive behavior support: Building systems to develop and maintain appropriate social behavior. In C. M. Evertson & C. S. Weinstein (Eds.), *Handbook of classroom management: Research, practice, and contemporary issues* (pp. 833–854). Mahwah, NJ: Lawrence Erlbaum Associates.

Lipka, J. (with Mohatt, G., & Ciulistet Group). (1998). *Transforming the culture of schools: Yup'ik Eskimo examples.* Mahwah, NJ: Lawrence Erlbaum Associates.

Los Angeles Unified School District. (n.d.). *Organizing and managing the classroom environment* [Ed 201 course syllabus]. Retrieved September 18, 2006, from http://www.lausd.k12.ca.us/lausd/offices/di/ele_docs/ClassManagment/Class_Mgmt_Syllabus.doc

Lotan, R. A. (2006). Managing groupwork in the heterogeneous classroom. In C. M. Evertson & C. S. Weinstein (Eds.), *Handbook of classroom management: Research, practice, and contemporary issues* (pp. 525–539). Mahwah, NJ: Lawrence Erlbaum Associates.

Markus, H., & Kitayama, S. (1991). Culture and the self: Implications for cognition, emotion, and motivation. *Psychological Review, 98,* 224–253.

Markus, H. R., & Lin, L. R. (1999). Conflictways: Cultural diversity and the meanings and practices of conflict. In D. A. Prentice & D. T. Miller (Eds.), *Cultural divides: Understanding and overcoming group conflict.* New York: Russell Sage Foundation.

Marzano, R. J. (2003). *Classroom management that works: Research-based strategies for every teacher.* Alexandria, VA: Association for Supervision and Curriculum Development.

Maslow, A. (1970). *Motivation and personality.* New York: Harper & Row.

Maynard, A. E. (2002). Cultural teaching: The development of teaching skills in Zinacantec Maya sibling interactions. *Child Development, 73*(3), 969–982.

McAlpine, L., & Taylor, D. (1993). Instructional preferences of Cree, Inuit, and Mohawk teachers. *Journal of American Indian Education, 33,* (1), 1–20.

McCaleb, S. P. (1995). *Building communities of learners: A collaboration among teachers, students, families, and community.* Mahwah, NJ: Lawrence Erlbaum Associates.

McCarthy, J., & Benally, J. (2003). Classroom management in a Navajo middle school. *Theory into Practice, 42* (4), 296-304.

McCaslin, M., Bozack, A. R., Napoleon, L., Thomas, A., Vasquez, V., Wayman, V., et al. (2006). Self-regulated learning and classroom management: Theory, research and considerations for classroom practice. In C. M. Evertson & C. S. Weinstein (Eds.), *Handbook of classroom management: Research, practice, and contemporary issues* (pp. 223–252). Mahwah, NJ: Lawrence Erlbaum Associates.

McLaughlin, H. J., & Bryan, L. A. (2003, Autumn). Learning from rural Mexican schools about commitment and work. *Theory into Practice, 42*(4), 289–295.

McLeod, J., Fisher, J., & Hoover, G. (2003). *The key elements of classroom management.* Alexandria, VA: Association for Supervision and Curriculum Development.

McNeil, L. M. (2000). Creating new inequalities: Contradictions of reform. *Phi Delta Kappan, 81*(10), 729–734.

Meier, D. (2000). *Will standards save public education?* Boston: Beacon Press.

Moles, O. (1996). *Reaching all families: Creating family-friendly schools.* Washington, DC: Office of Educational Research and Improvement.

Moll, L. C., & Gonzalez, N. (2004). Engaging life: A funds-of-knowledge approach to multicultural education. In J. Banks & C. A. McGee Banks (Eds.), *Handbook of research on multicultural education* (pp. 699–715). San Francisco: Jossey-Bass.

Morine-Dershimer, G. (2006). Classroom management and classroom discourse. In C. M. Evertson & C. S. Weinstein (Eds.), *Handbook of classroom management: Research, practice, and contemporary issues* (pp. 127–153). Mahwah, NJ: Lawrence Erlbaum Associates.

Morrow, L. M., Reutzel, D. R., & Casey, H. (2006). Organization and management of language arts teaching: Classroom environments, grouping practices, and exemplary instruction. In C. M. Evertson & C. S. Weinstein (Eds.), *Handbook of classroom management: Research, practice, and contemporary issues* (pp. 559–581). Mahwah, NJ: Lawrence Erlbaum Associates.

Mosier, C. E., & Rogoff, B. (2003). Privileged treatment of toddlers: Cultural aspects of individual choice and responsibility. *Developmental Psychology, 39*(6), 1047–1060.

Nelson-Barber, S., & Dull, V. (1998). Don't act like a teacher! Images of effective instruction in a Yup'ik Eskimo classroom. In J. Lipka, with G. V. Mohatt & The Ciulistet Group. *Transforming the culture of schools: Yup'ik Eskimo examples* (pp. 91–105). Mahwah, NJ: Lawrence Erlbaum Associates.

Nelson-Barber, S., Trumbull, E., & Wenn, R. (2000). *The coconut wireless project: Sharing culturally responsive pedagogy through the world wide web.* Honolulu, HI: Pacific Resources for Education and Learning.

Nelson-LeGall, S., & Resnick, L. (1998). Help seeking, achievement motivation, and the social practice of intelligence in school. In S. A. Karabenick (Ed.) *Strategic help seeking: Implications for learning and teaching* (pp. 39–60). Mahwah, NJ: Lawrence Erlbaum Associates.

Nieto, S. (1998). Fact and fiction: Stories of Puerto Ricans in U.S. schools. *Harvard Educational Review, 68*(2), 133–163.

Nieto, S. (1999). *The light in their eyes: Creating multicultural learning communities.* New York: Teachers College Press.

Noll, E. (1994). Social issues and literature circles with adolescents. *Journal of Reading, 38,* 88–93.

Nsamenang, A. B., & Lamb, M. E. (1994). Socialization of Nso children in the Bamenda grassfields of Northwest Cameroon. In P. M. Greenfield & R. R. Cocking (Eds.), *Cross-cultural roots of minority child development* (pp. 133–146). Hillsdale, NJ: Lawrence Erlbaum Associates.

Nucci, L. (2006). Classroom management for moral and social development. In C. M. Evertson, & C. S. Weinstein, (Eds.) *Handbook of classroom management: Research, practice, and contemporary issues* (pp. 711–731). Mahwah, NJ: Lawrence Erlbaum Associates.

O'Donnell, A. M. (2006). The role of peers and group learning. In P. A. Alexander & P. H. Winne (Eds.), *Handbook of educational psychology* (2nd ed., pp. 781–802). Mahwah, NJ: Lawrence Erlbaum Associates.

Ohanian, S. (2001). News from the test resistance trail. *Phi Delta Kappan, 82*(5), 363–366.

Osterman, K. F. (2000). Students' need for belonging in the school community. *Review of Educational Research, 70*(23), 323–367.

Padilla, A. M. (2002). Hispanic psychology: A 25-year retrospective look. In W. J. Lonner, D. I. Dinnel, S. A. Hayes, & D. N. Sattler (Eds.), *Online readings in psychology and culture* (Unit 3, Chapter 3). Bellingham, WA: Center for Cross-Cultural Research, Western Washington University.

Palincsar, A. S., & Brown, A. L. (1984). Reciprocal teaching of comprehension-fostering and comprehension-monitoring activities. *Cognition and Instruction, 1,* 117–175.

Paradise, R. (2002). Finding ways to study culture in context. *Human Development, 45,*(4), 229–236.

Pearson, P. D., & Duke, N. K. (2002). Comprehension instruction in the primary grades. In C. C. Block & M. Pressley (Eds.), *Comprehension instruction: Research-based best practices* (pp. 247–258). New York: Guilford Press.

Piaget, J. (1952). *The origins of intelligence in children* (M. Cook, Trans.). New York: International University Press.

Pianta, R. C. (2006). Classroom management and relationships between children and teachers: Implications for research and practice. In C. M. Evertson & C. S. Weinstein (Eds.), *Handbook of classroom management: Research, practice, and contemporary issues* (pp. 685–709). Mahwah, NJ: Lawrence Erlbaum Associates.

Pianta, R. C., & Cox, M. J. (1999). *The transition to kindergarten.* Baltimore: Paul Brooks Publishing.

Pianta, R. C., Cox, M. J., Taylor, L., & Early, D. (1999). Kindergarten teachers' practices related to the transition to school: Results from a national survey. *The Elementary School Journal, 100* (1) 71–86.

Popham, W. J. (2003). Preparing for the coming avalanche of accountability tests. In Editors of the *Harvard Education Letter* (Eds.), *Spotlight on high-stakes testing* (pp. 9–15). Cambridge, MA: Harvard Education Press.

Quiroz, B., & Greenfield, P. M. (1996). *Cross-cultural value conflict: Removing a barrier to Latino school achievement.* Unpublished manuscript.

Quiroz, B., Greenfield, P. M., & Altchech, M. (1999, April). Bridging cultures with a parent-teacher conference. *Educational Leadership, 56*(7), 69–70.

Raeff, C. (1997). Individuals in relationships: Cultural values, children's social interactions, and the development of an American individualistic self. *Developmental Review, 17,* 205–238.

Raeff, C., Greenfield, P. M., & Quiroz, B. (2000). Conceptualizing interpersonal relationships in the cultural contexts of individualism and collectivism. In S. Harkness, C. Raeff, & C. M. Super (Eds.), *New directions for child and adolescent development, 87.* San Francisco: Jossey-Bass.

Reese, L., Balzano, S., Gallimore, R., & Goldenberg, C. (1995). The concept of *educación:* Latino family values and American schooling. *International Journal of Educational Research, 23*(1), 57–81.

Robinson, S. L., & Ricord Griesemer, S. M. (2006). Helping individual students with problem behavior. In C. M. Evertson & C. S. Weinstein (Eds.), *Handbook of classroom management: Research, practice, and contemporary issues* (pp. 787–802). Mahwah, NJ: Lawrence Erlbaum Associates.

Rogoff, B. (2003). *The cultural nature of human development.* Oxford, England: Oxford University Press.

Roman, L. (2006). *Bridging cultures: Taking a look at independence and interdependence among high school students.* Unpublished master's thesis, California State University, Northridge.

Rothstein-Fisch, C. (2003). *Bridging Cultures teacher education module.* Mahwah, NJ: Lawrence Erlbaum Associates.

Rothstein-Fisch, C., Trumbull, E., Isaac, A., Daley, C., & Pérez, A. I. (2003). When "helping someone else" is the right answer: Bridging Cultures in assessment. *Journal of Latinos and Education, 2*(3), 123–140.

Salas, L. (2004). Individualized educational plan (IEP) meetings and Mexican American parents: Let's talk about it. *Journal of Latinos and Education, 3*(3), 181–192.

Santrock, J. W. (2004). *Educational psychology* (2nd ed.). Boston: McGraw-Hill.

Sarason, S. (1971). *The culture of school and the problem of change.* Boston: Allyn & Bacon.

Scarpaci, R. T. (2007). *A case study approach to classroom management.* Boston: Pearson/Allyn & Bacon.

Schaps, E. (2003, March). Creating a school community. *Educational Leadership, 60*(6), 31–33.

Sergiovanni, T. (1994). *Building community in our schools.* San Francisco: Jossey-Bass.

Sheets, R. (1999). Relating competence in an urban classroom to ethnic identity development. In R. Sheets (Ed.), *Racial and ethnic identity in school practices: Aspects of human development.* Mahwah, NJ: Lawrence Erlbaum Associates.

Sheets, R. H. (2005). *Diversity pedagogy: Examining the role of culture in the teaching-learning process.* Boston: Pearson Education.

Shore, B. (2002). Taking culture seriously. *Human Development, 45*(4), 226–228.

Slavin, R. (1990). *Cooperative learning: Theory, research, and practice.* Boston: Allyn & Bacon.

Slavin, R. E. (2006). *Educational psychology: Theory and practice* (8th ed.). Boston: Pearson.

Solano-Flores, G., & Trumbull, E. (2003). Examining language in context: The need for new research and practice paradigms in the testing of English language learners. *Educational Researcher, 32*(2), 3–13.

Solano-Flores, G., Trumbull, E., & Nelson-Barber, S. (2002). Concurrent development of dual language assessments: An alternative to translating tests for linguistic minorities. *International Journal of Testing, 2*(2), 107–129.

Sosa, A. S. (1997). Involving Hispanic parents in educational activities through collaborative relationships. *Bilingual Research Journal, 21*(2&3), 1–8.

Stiggins, R. J. (1997). *Student-centered classroom assessment* (2nd ed.). Upper Saddle River, NJ: Merrill.

Tapia Uribe, F. M., LeVine, R. A., & LeVine, S. E. (1994). Maternal behavior in a Mexican community: The changing environments of children. In P. M. Greenfield & R. R. Cocking (Eds.), *Cross-cultural roots of minority child development* (pp. 41–54). Hillsdale, NJ: Lawrence Erlbaum Associates.

Tharp, R. G., Estrada, P., Dalton, S. S., & Yamauchi, L. A. (2000). *Teaching transformed: Achieving excellence, fairness, inclusion, and harmony.* Boulder, CO: Westview.

Triandus, H. C. (1989). Cross-cultural studies of individualism and collectivism. *Nebraska Symposium of Motivation, 37*, 43–133.

Trumbull, E. (2000). Why do we grade—and should we? In E. Trumbull & B. Farr (Eds.) *Grading and reporting student progress in an age of standards* (pp. 23–43). Norwood, MA: Christopher-Gordon.

Trumbull, E. (2005). Language, culture, and society. In E. Trumbull & B. Farr, *Language and learning: What teachers need to know* (pp. 33–72). Norwood, MA: Christopher-Gordon.

Trumbull, E., Diaz-Meza, R., & Hasan, A. (2000, April). *Bridging Cultures in literacy practices.* Paper presented at the annual meeting of the American Educational Research Association, New Orleans.

Trumbull, E., Diaz-Meza, R., Hasan, A., & Rothstein-Fisch, C. (2001).*The Bridging Cultures Project Five-Year Report: 1996–2000.* San Francisco: WestEd. Available: http://www.wested. org/bridging/BC_5yr_report.pdf

Trumbull, E., Greenfield, P. M., & Quiroz, B. (2003). Cultural values in learning and education. In B. Williams (Ed.), *Closing the achievement gap: A vision for changing beliefs and practices* (2nd ed., pp. 67–98). Alexandria, VA: Association for Supervision and Curriculum Development.

Trumbull, E., Greenfield, P. M., Rothstein-Fisch, C., & Maynard, A. (1999, April). *From altered perceptions to altered practice: Teachers bridge cultures in the classroom.* Paper presented at the annual meeting of the American Educational Research Association, Montréal, Quebec.

Trumbull, E., & Koelsch, N. (in press). Developing a district-wide reading assessment for students in transition. In M. del R. Basterra & G. Solano-Flores (Eds.), *Language, culture, and assessment.* Baltimore: Mid-Atlantic Equity Center.

Trumbull, E., & Koelsch, N. (under review). Reading assessment for bilingual students in transition.

Trumbull, E., & Pacheco, M. (2005). *The teacher's guide to diversity: Building a knowledge base.* Providence, RI: Education Alliance at Brown University.

Trumbull, E., Rothstein-Fisch, C., & Greenfield, P. M. (2000). *Bridging cultures in our schools: New approaches that work* [Knowledge brief]. San Francisco: WestEd.

Trumbull, E., Rothstein-Fisch, C., Greenfield, P. M., & Quiroz, B. (2001). *Bridging cultures between home and school: A guide for teachers.* Mahway, NJ: Lawrence Erlbaum Associates.

Trumbull, E., Rothstein-Fisch, C., & Hernandez, E. (2003). Parent involvement-According to whose values? *School Community Journal, 13*(2), 45–72.

Valdés, G. (1996). *Con respeto: Bridging the distances between culturally diverse families and schools, an ethnographic portrait.* New York: Teachers College Press.

Valdés, G., & Figueroa, R. (1994). *Bilingualism and testing: A special case of bias.* Norwood, NJ: Ablex Publishing Company.

Valencia, R. R., & Solórzano, D. G. (1997). Contemporary deficit thinking. In R. R. Valencia (Ed.), *The evolution of deficit thinking: Educational thought and practice* (pp. 160–210). London: Falmer Press.

Valenzuela, A. (1999). *Subtractive schooling: U.S.-Mexican youth and the politics of caring.* Albany, NY: SUNY Press.

Vygotsky, L. (1986). *Thought and language* (Rev. ed.). Cambridge, MA: MIT Press.

Walker, J. M. T., & Hoover-Dempsey, K. V. (2006). Why research on parental involvement is important to classroom management. In C. M. Evertson & C. S. Weinstein (Eds.), *Handbook of classroom management: Research, practice, and contemporary issues* (pp. 665–684). Mahwah, NJ: Lawrence Erlbaum Associates.

Waltman, J. L., & Bush-Bacelis, J. L. (1995). Contrasting expectations of individualists and collectivists: Achieving effective group interaction. *Journal of Teaching in International Business, 7*(1), 61–76.

Watson, M., & Battistich, V. (2006). Building and sustaining caring communities. In C. M. Evertson & C. S. Weinstein (Eds.), *Handbook of classroom management: Research, practice, and contemporary issues* (pp. 253–279). Mahwah, NJ: Lawrence Erlbaum Associates.

Webb, N. M. (1991). Task-related verbal interaction and mathematics learning in small groups. *Journal of Research in Mathematics Education, 22*, 366–369.

Weinstein, C. S. (2003). Classroom management in a diverse society. *Theory into Practice, 42*(4), 266–268.

Weinstein, C., Curran, M., & Tomlinson-Clarke, S. (2003). Culturally responsive classroom management: Awareness into action. *Theory into Practice, 42*(4), 269–276.

Weinstein, C. S., & Mignano, A. J. (2003). *Elementary classroom management: Lessons from research and practice* (3rd ed.). Boston: McGraw-Hill.

Wentzel, K. R. (2003). Motivating students to behave in socially competent ways. *Theory into Practice, 42* (4), 319–326.

Wentzel, K. R. (2006). A social motivation perspective for classroom management. In C. M. Evertson & C. S. Weinstein (Eds.), *Handbook of classroom management: Research, practice, and contemporary issues* (pp. 619–643). Mahwah, NJ: Lawrence Erlbaum Associates.

Whiting, B. B., & Whiting, J. M. W. (1975). *Children of six cultures: A psycho-cultural analysis.* Cambridge, MA: Harvard University Press.

INDEX

Note: Page references for figures are indicated with an *f* after the page numbers.

ABOUT THE AUTHORS

 Carrie Rothstein-Fisch

Carrie Rothstein-Fisch, PhD, is associate professor of Educational Psychology and Counseling at California State University, Northridge. She is one of the four original researchers on the Bridging Cultures Project, a longitudinal action research project that explores ways to improve cross-cultural understanding and communication, particularly for Latino students and their families. She has authored or coauthored numerous articles and book chapters, and she is the author, coauthor, or editor of four other books on Bridging Cultures: *Bridging Cultures Between Home and School: A Guide for Teachers* (with Elise Trumbull, Patricia M. Greenfield, and Blanca Quiroz, 2001); *Bridging Cultures Teacher Education Module* (2003); *Readings for Bridging Cultures Teacher Education Module* (2003); and *Bridging Cultures in Early Care and Education* (with Marlene Zepeda, Janet Gonzalez-Mena, and Elise Trumbull, 2006).

Rothstein-Fisch received her PhD in Educational Psychology and Developmental Studies from UCLA. She earned the Distinguished Teaching Award at California State University, Northridge. She can be contacted at the Michael D. Eisner College of Education, California State University, Northridge, 18111 Nordhoff Street, Northridge, CA 91331-8265; or via e-mail at managingdiverseclassrooms@csun.edu.

Elise Trumbull

Elise Trumbull, EdD, is an educational consultant specializing in sociocultural influences on learning and schooling and a lecturer at California State University, Northridge, where she teaches a graduate course in Language and Concept Development in the department of Educational Psychology and Counseling. A former special education teacher, Trumbull completed her doctorate in education in the area of applied psycholinguistics at Boston University in 1984. She has studied seven languages other than English and has conducted applied research in cultural settings ranging from California, New York, Florida, and Arizona, to Micronesia.

Dr. Trumbull was the project director and an original researcher on the Bridging Cultures Project. She has coauthored dozens of articles and book chapters, as well as six books. Among them are *Assessment Alternatives for Diverse Classrooms* (with Beverly Farr, 1997); *Bridging Cultures Between Home and School: A Guide for Teachers* (with Carrie Rothstein-Fisch, Patricia M. Greenfield, and Blanca Quiroz, 2001); *Language and Learning: What Teachers Need to Know* (with Beverly Farr, 2000); and *The Teacher's Guide to Diversity: Building a Knowledge Base* (with Maria Pachecho, 2005). Dr. Trumbull can be reached at managingdiverseclassrooms@comcast.net.

Related ASCD Resources: Classroom Management and Diversity

At the time of publication, the following ASCD resources were available. For the most up-to-date information about ASCD resources, go to www.ascd.org. ASCD stock numbers are noted in parentheses.

Audio

Best Practices in Serving Gifted Hispanic Students by Jaime Castellano (Audiotape: #204202)

English Language Learners in the Mainstream: Strategies That Work by Virginia Rojas (Audiotape: #203100)

Succeeding in Diverse and Inclusive Schools (CD: #507127)

Mixed Media

Educating Linguistically and Culturally Diverse Students Professional Inquiry Kit by Belinda Williams (eight activity folders and a videotape) (#998060)

Networks

Visit the ASCD Web site (www.ascd.org) and click on About ASCD and then on Networks for information about professional educators who have formed groups around topics, including "Hispanic/Latino-American Critical Issues." Look in the "Network Directory" for current facilitators' addresses and phone numbers.

Print Products

Educating Everybody's Children: Diverse Teaching Strategies for Diverse Learners by Robert W. Cole (#195024)

Educational Leadership, March 2007, Responding to Changing Demographics (Entire Issue #107031)

Educational Leadership, October 2002, The World in the Classroom (Entire Issue #102306)

Fifty Strategies for Teaching English Language Learners, 2nd Edition by Adrienne Herrell and Michael Jordan (#303383)

Getting Started with English Language Learners: How Educators Can Meet the Challenge by Judie Haynes (#106048)

Meeting the Needs of Second Language Learners: An Educator's Guide by Judith Lessow-Hurley (#102043S25)

Videos and DVDs

Educating Everybody's Children (six 20- to 30-minute videotapes and two facilitator's guides) (#400228)

How to Coteach to Meet Diverse Student Needs (one 15-minute videotape) (#406057)

How to Involve All Parents in Your Diverse Community (one 15-minute DVD) (#607056)

For additional resources, visit us on the World Wide Web (http://www.ascd.org), send an e-mail message to member@ascd.org, call the ASCD Service Center (1-800-933-ASCD or 703-578-9600, then press 2), send a fax to 703-575-5400, or write to Information Services, ASCD, 1703 N. Beauregard St., Alexandria, VA 22311-1714 USA.